P9-ARU-816

Performing Television

Performing Television:
Contemporary Drama
and the Media Culture

Elizabeth Klaver

Bowling Green State University Popular Press
Bowling Green, OH 43403

Library of Congress Cataloging-in-Publication Data
Klaver, Elizabeth.
    Performing television: contemporary drama and the media cul-
ture / Elizabeth Klaver.
        p.   cm.
    Includes bibliographical references and index.
    ISBN 0-87972-825-6 (cloth). -- ISBN 0-87972-826-4 (pbk.)
        1. Television and theater. 2. American drama--20th century
--History and criticism. 3. Television in literature. 4. Television
broadcasting--Social aspects. I. Title.

PN1992.65.K59 2001
812'.609--dc21
                                                        00-050365

Cover design by Chris Carnicom

To the memory of my father,

Randy Klaver

CONTENTS

Acknowledgments   *ix*

Introduction   1

1 A Question of Subjectivity   25

2 The Mediatized Imaginary and the Critical Subject

    Position   53

3 Performing Television/Theorizing Performance   83

4 Televisual Sex and Violence   111

Conclusion   135

Index   139

ACKNOWLEDGMENTS

I would like to thank Southern Illinois University Carbondale, the English Department, and the Office of Research and Development at SIUC for their generous research support, which provided release time and grant funds. I could not have done this project without the help of my research assistants: Annie Natoli recovered many of the plays necessary for this study; and Chris Carlson resolutely worked through more than seventy years of articles on drama and the media.

A very special thanks goes to the students of my graduate seminars on drama and the media culture, especially those who participated in the workshop production of *Hamletmachine*: Marcy Chvasta, April Gentry, Mara Hatfield, Ryan Hibbert, Rob Howard, John Kavanaugh, Anne-Marie Obilade, Becky Plaza, Robin Roberts, Hong Wang, and Eva White. I would like to remember a particularly talented student, Andrew Smith, whose untimely death was a great loss.

I have many colleagues to thank for their reading of the manuscript and sound advice: Edward J. Brunner, Paula B. Bennett, Michael L. Humphries, R. Gerald Nelms, Steven Gould Axelrod, Terry L. Spaise, and Kevin J. H. Dettmar, to name just a few. I owe an enormous debt of gratitude to Ray B. Browne and Pat Browne for their expert guidance.

I am really grateful to my family for their astute observations of television and contemporary North American culture: my mother, Iris, my brothers, Brian and Bruce, and my husband, Mike.

INTRODUCTION

In the last scene of Tennessee Williams's *The Glass Menagerie*, Jim, the gentleman caller, explains to Laura his reason for taking classes in radio engineering and public speaking: "Because I believe in the future of television!" (100). Made in a play that premiered in 1944, Jim's remark must be one of the earliest references in the history of drama to the latest arrival on the media scene. However much this line may reverberate with ironic meanings in the context of *The Glass Menagerie*, its prophetic vision has turned out to be accurate. Now we all believe in the future of television. What has been less clear is the future of drama and its performance in the theater.

With television so clearly dominating the entertainment industry throughout the latter half of the twentieth century, those who are involved in the dramatic arts—from the playwrights, directors, and actors to the critics, scholars, and audiences—have been pressed to reconsider continually the future of drama. Of course, this is not a situation peculiar to drama and theater alone. The pervasive presence and power of television—which Fredric Jameson links to video as the cultural dominant of our time (69)—demand from every other cultural phenomenon from fiction and film to politics and toys a constant renegotiation of subject position, of identity, even of viability. The question comes down to whether we can consider any genre, indeed any cultural product, and its durability without acknowledging the weight of television and its position in the media culture.

Performing Television specifically interrogates how a negotiation for identity, even survivability, in the media culture occurs in one particular genre and cultural institution—postmodern drama and its performance in the theater. Is theater a viable performative art form given the overpowering presence of television? Is there an audience for drama when theater has given over to television and film the role it once played as popular entertainment? What sort of attraction can drama have to a

1

culture increasingly mesmerized by the televisual image? Is there a place for postmodern drama, even as the territory of the avant-garde, when television has become the main purveyor of culture? And how does drama deal with the ontological and epistemological challenges television is capable of making to time-honored performative "grounds." In short, how does contemporary drama meet the issue of its own identity, its subjectivity, in a postmodern media culture?

As the structuralist Mary Douglas points out in *Purity and Danger,* one way to handle the anomalies that arise in a culture is to ignore them (38). At times, especially during the immediate post–World War II years, drama has taken this approach to television, attempting to ignore the newcomer or at least keep it well separated and pretending that the media culture does not concern it. Jerzy Grotowski's *Poor Theater* is a good example of how a theater can be built upon a rejection of the "technical plant" of multi-media staging. And there is a certain attractiveness to such a strategy which is based upon the notion that theatrical practice is powerful enough to survive on its own without pandering to the mass media, giving in to gimmicks, or hopping on the bandwagon of multi-media performance. After all, one could say, theater has unique attributes that ought to be enough—the sense of special occasion, the community of audience, the magnetism of ritual, the vulnerability of live performance.

Yet there are several conditions that make such a purist and essentially modernist stance virtually impossible. As Andreas Huyssen points out in *After the Great Divide,* the exclusionary stance of modernism is precisely the best indicator of its dependence on popular or mass culture, "mass culture indeed seem[ing] to be the repressed other of modernism, the family ghost rumbling in the cellar" (16). More practically speaking, a great number of plays and productions that appear to have nothing to do with television or the media culture actually make reference to it. *The Glass Menagerie,* above, is a case in point. The purity of theater is already "contaminated" by television, because as cultural institutions both exist in the same postmodern world. The shredding of boundaries so often discussed as a feature of the postmodern is never so clearly evidenced as in the three-way configuration of theater, television, and film, performative genres that not only compete for similar audiences but also experience a constant crossover of actors, writers, directors, and material. In fact, theater departments are still the main training venue for actors in all the visual media. And finally, theater can never be completely differentiated from the other media simply because it is a medium itself, and as such is always involved in the circulation of images, messages, and information characteristic of late-twentieth-century culture.

Moreover, there are a surprising number of plays having been written and premiered since the mid-1960s that more directly respond to the question of the place of contemporary drama in the media culture by interrogating television and the various issues that arise when these two cultural forms meet. Oftentimes, the response is situated in the background of a play and occurs in references to television as a historical, cultural, or tropological signpost. For instance, the argument between Troy and Cory in August Wilson's *Fences* over buying a television set not only historically contextualizes the play in the late 1950s, but also provides information about contemporaneous African-American culture and acts as a metonymy for postwar economic advancement.

At other times, the response is located in the foreground, where a play may examine a thematic issue linked to television—its disassociation from reality, for instance, as in David Rabe's *Sticks and Bones*—or actually emplace television in the theater site by employing onstage TV monitors with closed-circuit viewing capacity or taped material and cameras. The use of TV monitors to deliver a soap-operatic version of Thornton Wilder's *Our Town* in the Wooster Group's *Route 1 & 9 (The Last Act)* is a good example. And sometimes the response is embedded in a profound televisual permeation in which a play simulates the structural and semiotic functions of television. *Coming Attractions* by Ted Tally, Jack Feldman, and Bruce Sussman, which I discuss further toward the end of the Introduction, bases its formal structure on an imitation of the way television's megatext functions over a block of viewing time with a variety of TV "advertisements" and other TV texts and images continually interrupting the play's main narrative line.

When plays such as these include to one degree or another instances of televisual discourse, they begin to expose the enormous difficulty of sorting out the relation of drama and theater to television and the media culture in general. The question goes deep into the structural foundations. Even though the stage and screen use similar semiotic, visual, and performative elements, their representational systems are quite different. There is a great contrast, for instance, between a live performance and a taped one. Never simply translatable as one set of signifiers to another (as a play performed on television might appear to be), when these two representational systems come together, even in the most innocent manner, they produce collisions and entanglements of a highly complex, often ambiguous nature which involves issues all the way from the ontological to the epistemological. To apply to theater and television Bert O. States's phenomenological analysis of the actor, the representational systems can be figured as "sphere[s] revolving in space" (373), but since space as well as time is handled differently in the two media, they revolve at different "RPMs."

In a very real sense, theater and television have different "chronotopes," M. M. Bakhtin's notion of how time and space connect in literary works (84). While many factors contribute to this distinction, perhaps the most obvious is the difference between their performance/audience chronotopes. Theater relies on a space-time proximity where the performance and audience occupy a simultaneous place and moment. Television, on the other hand, operates on a space-time discontinuity, where the viewed is always separated from the viewer by electronic beams of light if not by great distance and time as well. Certainly, any play that employs television apparatus on stage necessarily raises questions about such foundations as chronotopes and what happens when they intersect. *Hamletmachine* by Heiner Müller, for instance, in deploying television monitors at the same time as live performance, invites an inquiry into principles regarding "present" time and pastness, "present" world and absent, as well as the binaries of real and taped bodies, live and taped action. The fact that theater and television do not fit particularly well ontologically suggests some fundamental near misses: they construct worlds, but construct them differently; they represent worlds, but represent them differently; they know worlds, but know them differently.

In addition to the structural level, the sort of drama that deals with television also broaches a dizzying profusion of formal, social, and cultural issues, and ranges widely through a spectrum of critical positionings. One play may savage television as a cultural contaminant, while another may treat it as a nostalgic dreamscape. One play may criticize television's commodification of images, while another may celebrate its postmodernist style. One play may scoff at television's peculiar gaze or system of looks, while another may rally those same looks in the service of deconstructing ideology. One play may appeal to television as a realist icon, while another may employ it expressionistically.[1] As is most often the case, plays include a cluster of such positionings so that the response to television and the media culture becomes highly ambiguous and often ambivalent. For instance, *The Tommy Allen Show* written by Megan Terry in 1970 contests the superficial geniality of television but at the same time celebrates its structure and style.

And finally, whenever plays take up issues about television they inevitably take up issues about drama and theater, a theoretical position I develop at greater length in Chapter 1. Whether this phenomenon occurs self-consciously or unconsciously, the commentary on television at all levels—from the structural to the cultural—always rebounds to a self-commentary about the play and the performance. In part, this situation arises out of the near misses and entanglements involved in the collision of the two representational systems, which makes it impossible for theater to separate clearly the televisual discourse from its own. But it also arises because the play is always its own subject. As Marshall McLuhan points out, "When one medium uses another, it is the user that is the 'content'"; he gives the following example: a movie aired on television always becomes television content, a television movie if you will (280). In the theater, a play's use of television generates a self-reflexive act in which dramatic art itself ironically becomes the focus of attention.

To what extent this act of self-reflection is in control or not contributes yet a further complicating dimension to understanding the relation of drama to television. For instance, the rage directed against the media culture as a sort of ideological body snatcher in the 1970 *AC/DC* by Heathcote Williams recoils in barely controllable Artaudian cruelty against the live action itself. Analyzed more extensively in Chapter 4, this play erupts in violence both as action and interrogation. On the other hand, *Coming Attractions* manages to stay in control while conducting a bristling critique of dramatic performance by reverberating it through the televisual discourse. In defining character as nothing more than a media-manufactured image, this play demonstrates at the same time the dependence of that construct on the theatrical trade of the actor, while using an actor to produce the whole thing. While it accuses television of being market-driven, fad-driven, star-driven, sentimental, and violent, *Coming Attractions* says all of this about theater at the same time.

Recognizing that drama is the object of its own vexed interrogations of television means that the question of its subjectivity in a postmodern media culture is ultimately at stake. Is it possible to rethink a genre and cultural institution in terms of its having something like a subjectivity, something like a sense of self, coherent or otherwise? Is it reasonable to apply to a genre and cultural institution the theories of human subjectivity advanced by post-structuralists, phenomenologists, and performative theorists such as Judith Butler, Paul Smith, Jean-Paul Sartre, and Jacques Lacan? In a sense I am asking, without sounding parodic I hope, if it is possible to re-structuralize post-structuralism. I would argue that postmodern drama is in much the same position as the human subject with respect to the constructedness and performativity of identity as Butler contends about gender and the desire for whole selfhood as theorized by Lacan. If dramatic art wishes to realize identity, it must construct that identity in the light of some other, circulating desire through its lens. With all of the convolutions such a process suggests, television can play the role of that other.

Accordingly, the purpose of this book is to discuss the ways postmodern drama has been negotiating subjectivity with respect to television and, by extension, a place in the media culture in the last decades of the twentieth century. The plays included belong to what is considered the genre of contemporary drama—single-authored works existing in text form as well as production—by such authors as Samuel Beckett, Tennessee Williams, Michael Frayn, Jane Chambers, Megan Terry, Lee Blessing, Don DeLillo, Heiner Müller, Philip Kan Gotanda, Luis Valdez, Suzanne Maynard, and Rosalyn Drexler among others. It does not cover video, performance art, avantgarde direction, or multi-media staging, superb treatments of which may be found in Timothy Murray's *Drama Trauma*, Johannes Birringer's *Theatre, Theory, Postmodernism*, David Savran's *The Wooster Group, 1975-1985: Breaking the Rules*, and Margaret Morse's *Virtualities*. Similarly, it does not cover the influence of theater on television per se, a topic upon which exist many fine books, such as Martin Esslin's *Mediations* and *The Age of Television*. Rather, this book attempts to turn the tables, exploring the influence of television on plays (and productions), and is concerned less with themes than with structural, formal, ideological, cultural, social and philosophical issues.

The balance of this introduction illustrates through a reading of Tally's *Coming Attractions* the complexity and ambivalence found in positions taken toward television by many contemporary plays and sets the stage for topics ongoing throughout the book.[2] Chapter 1 generates the theoretical framework by articulating the subjectifying processes drama and production undergo in interrogating televisual discourse. Chapter 2 demonstrates how a critical subject position is constructed to contest the media culture, particularly the mediatized Imaginary. Chapter 3 shows how a theoretical subject position is generated when the televisual discourse performed on stage comments on the semiosis, performativity, and spectatorship of theater. And Chapter 4, in focusing on the hot-button topic of sex and violence on television, argues that the dramatic and media arts share a similar ideological identity and political position as the objects of a disciplinary society.

Coming Attractions

Since the early 1970s critical attention has regularly turned to the rising significance of the visual media and their effect on contemporary Western culture. Raymond Williams and Marshall McLuhan made important early contributions to cultural criticism and television studies by taking seriously the way media work and their impact on viewers. More recently, major drama critics such as Herbert Blau, Timothy Murray, and Johannes Birringer consider the place of dramatic art with respect to the newer, more popular forms of visual entertainment. An ongoing topic concerns the function of "high culture" theater, video, and performance art in a media culture where image-making, commodification, and questions of subjectivity and spectatorship are rupturing all sorts of notions about drama. In *Theatre, Theory, Postmodernism*, for instance, Birringer emphasizes the connection between postmodern culture, theory, and contemporary theater practice and argues for the reinvention of a drama that could acknowledge a complex multicultural society (x-xi).

Coming Attractions (book by Ted Tally, music by Jack Feldman, and lyrics by Feldman and Bruce Sussman) provides an exemplary moment to reconsider the place of drama in the postmodern era, a time characterized by the proliferation of media and information systems as well as by a general trend toward fragmentation and decentralization. First performed during the 1980 season at Playwrights Horizons in New York, *Coming Attractions* is a darkly humorous play about the rise to celebrity status of Lonnie, an aimless young man turned serial killer. The numerous murders he commits are designed by Manny, a theatrical agent, to combine crime and show business, to attract deliberately the attention of newspapers and cameras.

Most interesting, though, is the play's incorporation of Lonnie's story into a dramatic structure that is shaped like network television. The play replicates the hard, glittering images associated with game shows and the continually shifting array of scenes and dramatic units that flicker endlessly across the screen of the TV set. By inscribing the discourse of television into its dramatic form, *Coming Attractions* well demonstrates the ambivalence we find in the most complex of contemporary drama about television, a drama that enacts, often jubilantly, a media culture while opening up for critique a variety of problems currently at issue in it. At the same time, *Coming Attractions* also shows how plays can occupy an ironic subject position, for its appropriation of what Tally calls "the media circus" (Preface 275) indicates that theater as a cultural institution must be involved in the postmodern era.

Coming Attractions discovers much of its spirited playfulness precisely in the competing position it has as a play that functions as a performance of the media culture and as a contestation. Very often throughout its history, theater has served to critique and correct the social and political scene, directing its attention in the case of Tally's play toward television as the main proprietor among the media of images, commodities, and consumer desire. To be sure, one way of interpreting the play is to recognize Tally's attempt to satirize the popular media, its consumerism and sensationalism, from a high culture stance. As he writes in the preface, "Nothing sells soap bars . . . like someone else's personal tragedy" (275). Whether the play manages to fulfill a satiric role, though, is another matter. Reviewers of its New York opening, for instance, seem nervous about terming it a satire, preferring to describe the play as a "satiric farce" (Kalem 86), "a bit of extended cabaret with satiric intent," and as "a musical lampoon" (Oliver 80).

Such qualifications result from the way *Coming Attractions* on one level uses the story of Lonnie's meteoric rise to fame to lambaste the media culture, but on another level undercuts the satirical thrust by arranging its structure like the most popular of the media—television. For instance, the opening stage directions specifically evoke the atmosphere of a TV taping studio: "In its design, colors, textures, and 'feel,' [the setting] suggests the set for a TV game show—slick but soulless" (276). Chaser lights outlining the stage floor and walls generate the dazzle of a *Wheel of Fortune*. Simply incorporating the staging of television makes it impossible for the play thoroughly to distance itself from its satirical object; instead, it illustrates the impossibility of unpacking fully a system from the inside.

In fact, *Coming Attractions* has so much fun with its televisual features that it becomes virtually celebratory. A first glance clearly shows the play utilizing the superficial properties of television—the lights, the glitter, the music; a closer inspection, though, reveals a sophisticated reproduction of features of network televisual discourse. Most of the texts on television, whether situation comedies, news programs, or commercials, are constructed out of a rapidly shifting series of camera angles and shots and the juxtaposition of many brilliant images and short episodic scenes. While a barrage of mesmerizing sights and sounds may seem like a desperate way to structure a narrative, these principles are appropriate to a medium whose shows have to compete with many other programs airing at the same time on many channels.

As Raymond Williams points out, in contrast to a play or book, a television show never exists by itself (80-81). It is part of a vast megatext on network television, a complex I have elsewhere described as the twenty-four-hour, continuous delivery of programs, commercials, and channels as they play among each other (see my "Postmodernism and the Intersection of Television and Contemporary Drama" 69-72). Even television dramas that operate like conventional plays with beginning, middle, and end do not really have the structure or pace of theater plays. Each TV narrative is deliberately designed to be interrupted at the end of an episodic fragment, about every twelve minutes, so that five or six playlets—commercials—can air. If the viewer goes channel-surfing during the commercial break, becomes distracted by some other program in the megatext and fails to return, the notions of a well-made ending and dramatic integrity are inevitably skewed. Because it has been supplanted by a new text, the original program is left with the ability merely to gesture toward closure.

Coming Attractions provides the experience of watching a play act like television, because it attempts to perform the principles of structure dictated by televisual discourse. Assembled out of a nonstop barrage of short skits, the play runs straight through ninety minutes without letting up for the usual intermission of theater. One episodic scene (there are nineteen in all) bounces quickly to another, juxtaposing skit, character, image, and face. The audience observers what Jim Collins calls a "proliferation of signs" (331), a battery of hard-hitting, dramatic fragments—many of them "television shows"—that interrupt and replace one another as if they were the product of channel-surfing the megatext. While it does manage to stay on course, the story line seems dangerously vulnerable, the play distracted by its own violent interruptions. This television bricolage creates

the impression that *Coming Attractions* is about to self-decon-
struct. One senses it could shift its primary focus onto any
number of internal playlets—the Miss America Contest or a TV
news broadcast skit—leaving Lonnie's story permanently up in
the air. If the audience cannot relinquish a modernist expecta-
tion of deep structure and dramatic cohesion, the play's "schizophrenic writing," to use the term Fredric Jameson applies to
postmodernist fragmentation (26-29), will produce utter disori-
entation.

    Coming Attractions is able to simulate the structure of tele-
vision by cleverly using stage properties—the revolves and spin-
ning, sliding panels that allow rapid entry and scene alteration.
Segments of the play are made to interrupt or dissolve into each
other. Consider the following example. At one moment a news-
paper publisher is dictating headlines in his office—"Halloween
Fiend Stalks Jackie O!" At the next moment Lonnie machine-
guns him down. As the publisher spins through a panel, Manny
enters from a wing. He shouts at Lonnie, grabs the publisher's
chair and exits through an Up Right wing. At the same time,
Lonnie spins through a stage Left panel as a TV cameraman
appears and a reporter enters from an Up Left wing. They start a
television interview with the father of one of the victims (289-
90). This sort of rapid, disjointed transition between skits occurs
again and again, so that the play seems to perform the kind of
jump-cut television uses to traverse a series of dramatic units,
abruptly supplanting one scene with another.

    Much of the performance energy of *Coming Attractions*
comes from this rapid action of texts and images. By giving the
various actors multiple roles, the play can even replicate the
effect of exchange and repetition common to television advertisements. Except for the two actors playing Lonnie and Manny,
each cast member has from six to twelve parts. For instance, in
the 1980 performances at Playwrights Horizons, Jonathan
Hadary played the roles of a hostage, the second newsman, a
detective, a TV cameraman, Mister X, a psychiatrist, Sammy
Dazzle of the Sammy Dazzle talk show, a private eye, the
defense attorney, and the director of Lonnie's final television
appearance. Hadary's face repeated itself over and over but in
different contexts across the landscape of the play. To appreciate

the full impact of the multiple roles, though, one has to imagine all five secondary actors continually showing up in different contexts, rapidly exchanging character to weave a dramatic text that is paradoxically repetitious and unpredictable.

As the play progresses, the link to television becomes clearer, which offers a similar repetitive stream of faces all day long, particularly in its commercials. Television advertisements not only focus on the close-up shot, but continually recycle the same faces throughout the television day, in part by simply airing advertisements over and over. In addition, the actors may also appear in a variety of roles. A major midwestern bank, for instance, uses an actor who also promotes plastic storage bags and pesticide products. Or an advertiser may borrow a famous face from a particular setting—Candice Bergen is a good example—and relocate the image (Murphy Brown) in a new venue (Sprint spokesperson). As in *Coming Attractions*, the face stays the same, but character and setting change. Furthermore, these commercials are played throughout the television megatext, and can be inserted into whatever program happens to be airing, whether *Jeopardy* or *The Tonight Show*. As a result, the faces become ever more familiar, but recontextualized in new settings. (Sometimes recontextualization happens with disastrous results, as when frenetically happy Coke drinkers immediately follow a war news story.) Thus, a few hours of television viewing reveals a number of recognizable faces repeating themselves across an assortment of roles and contexts.

Coming Attractions replicates this televisual operation to much the same fascinating effect. Even though it is the director who casts the actors in the multiple roles, the faces seem to surface indiscriminately in a variety of skits and scenes, attachable to every context and to none, lacking depth or referent and infinitely manipulable. Like the faces in television advertisements, they flicker across the play as the pictorial representative of type, the icon of character rather than character, which subverts the phenomenological equation of actor with character so important to modernist drama. In plays that promote an essence of selfhood and being in their characters, the actor presents "sides" consistent with behavior that add up to a perception of completeness by the audience (see States 373). As the theatrical illusion develops, the gap between character and actor closes, so that eventually "roundness" is able to lend an abiding essence to the character. When the same actor presents one flat side of a variety of characters, however, the phenomenological equation is bound to short-circuit. While multiple roles will tend to subvert essentialist selfhood generally, the separation of actor from character in the televisual world of *Coming Attractions* produces the particular insight that an image (not an essentialist self) is moving across time, an image, moreover, that can be likened to Birringer's description of the "'role' of the performer" in technologized performance as being capable of random reproduction and distribution (177).

Disallowing the phenomenological illusion, a subject revisited at depth in Chapter 1, means that the way Manny and Lonnie are perceived is also affected, because they are played by actors who are competing with the stream of faces in the play's televisual field. They cannot be detached from a narrative that seems dangerously unstable, nor a semiotic "ground" that deconstructs the subject as a repetitive series of exchangeable, televisual images. Indeed, Lonnie is paraded across the landscape of the play as a number of media icons. Whereas modernist drama attempted to create the impression of a single, stable character, one whose coherence as a subject is continually asserted, it has been the project of postmodernist drama to break that down. *Coming Attractions* not only plays itself off televisual discourse, but enacts it as well, presenting a dramatic universe that is structured like television—fragmented, imagistic, unstable, unlimited, slick.

In fact, the play's remarkable effort to dramatize televisual structure through a complete reliance on theater principles makes it different from contemporaneous experiments in multi-media by the Wooster Group, Squat Theatre, and many performance artists of the 1980s and 1990s. Such work tends to explore the relation of live to taped performance by juxtaposing the hot medium of theater with the coolness of taped television. In *Coming Attractions,* by contrast, because there is no television apparatus on stage, theater is completely responsible for generating the impression of televisual structure and form. In many respects, *Coming Attractions* is comparable to Oliver Stone's 1994 film, *Natural Born Killers*, which also covers the rise to celebrity of serial killers. By incorporating television's laugh track, its rapid cutting from image to image, and its Saturday-morning cartoon figures, Stone's film makes a similar effort to replicate televisual discourse and to comment on the sort of world it produces. Nevertheless, such performance always has to return self-reflexively to the structuring principles of the grounding medium, whether film or theater. *Natural Born Killers*, for instance, demonstrating what I term "mis-regulation" in Chapter 4, uses its own glamorous images of violence to critique the glamorization of violence on television.

It is evident, then, that in order to enact television "images" *Coming Attractions* has to use theatrical images, a theoretical ground explored in Chapter 3. The play cannot step outside a system of signs, for a system of signs must generate the play. Rather than bracketing the opacity of one semiotics (television) with the transparency of the other (theater), all signs in the play begin to glow in the same glittering light. Therefore, televisual discourse demystifies not simply modernist essentialism, but the entire illusory apparatus of performative forms. Televisual discourse forces a recognition of the semiotic status of theatrical discourse, which makes it impossible for the play to wrap itself in an aesthetic of distance. As the effect of enacting television reverberates back onto the theater images, we are able to witness the shifting boundaries that Blau has seen occurring in art since the 1960s (*Audience* 60). In such a postmodern venue, the intent of satire, which must clearly distance its object of ridicule, is necessarily compromised. At the same time the play is making a performance of television, television is demonstrating how drama is postmodernized.

In other words, the play's demystification of theater apparatus and its obvious delight in television disrupt the subject position of a full-blown, high-culture satire, a pose that seems increasingly impossible in a postmodern age. To put it simply, the play cannot completely (or perhaps does not want to) separate itself from the media culture that it is attempting to critique. This involvement does not mean, however, that *Coming Attractions* is destroying itself by imitating television or that theater is losing significance to the mass media, as some drama practitioners fear. Despite its replication of televisual structure, the play operates in theater space and thus makes a performance of television, rather than ontologically "being" television.

In fact, *Coming Attractions* finds itself in the sort of liminal condition Linda Hutcheon describes as the doubleness of irony in a postmodern paradigm. Postmodern irony works on the principle that a discourse may be involved in a dominant culture, but able to indicate at the same time "a position of difference and even opposition" (14). Thus, *Coming Attractions* can admit that drama today operates in a postmodern age while continuing its cultural role of critical commentator on society. *Coming Attractions* uses its own television-saturated world to expose the way that a media culture constructs "reality," cultivates consumerism, and affects the individual subject.

Incorporating skits about all sorts of media sleaze, the play places Lonnie's rise to notoriety within a media-driven, consumer terrain. Manny pictures Lonnie's "career" entirely as product-oriented: "your face on *every*thing—tee shirts, posters, candy bars, *jogging* shorts. Sponsorship! Commercials! . . . More books! More films! A whole entertainment *empire*, based on the sequels to the novelizations of the rip-offs of the spin-offs of the albums of the mini-series!!!" (284). Interestingly, Manny's purpose as a theatrical agent is to reinvent Lonnie as a media star, a role that recalls the star system of theater and its commercialization of images, which is enhanced by the play's musical score and "Broadway" feel.

When Lonnie complains that he feels ridiculous outfitted in a Halloween skeleton costume, Manny convinces him that the crimes need to be "sexy." They need a "political thing," an "extra touch of mystery" (283). Indeed, TV news, as well as the rest of the media culture, notices Lonnie only when he does become theatrical, when he performs as "The Halloween Killer." Daniel C. Hallin explains that the news media not only combine journalism and the theatrics of show business, but thrive on a mixture of populism and crisis. On the one hand, TV news likes to focus on ordinary people, recognizing the streak of populism in North American culture and politics. On the other hand, it loves nothing more than a hostage situation (11-20). In Lonnie, the TV news finds a near-perfect combination: the contemporary populist hero who is both an ordinary person and its perversion, a figure like

David Berkowitz ("Son of Sam"), whom Tally admits in his preface influenced the play (275). Lonnie attracts the news media because he is the kind of commercial product they can invest with desirability.

According to Edward S. Herman and Noam Chomsky in *Manufacturing Consent*, the media are large corporations that are driven by "market-profit-oriented forces" (14), where advertisers exert enormous control over what kind of information and entertainment is offered to the public, an aspect of the disciplining function of ideology discussed in Chapter 4. In *Coming Attractions*, the TV News broadcast skit demonstrates this link between news information and the marketplace. With the News theme song playing behind them, the TV News team revolves on stage and addresses imaginary cameras, reporting on the latest victims of "The Halloween Killer." Lights direct attention to different areas of the stage, cutting from a reporter to the police chief, reproducing a director's switching among the videos of a news story. Commercial lead-ins by the team pull in seemingly random material from the megatext—"And now a word from Pit Stop, official deodorant of the Indianapolis 500!" (286).

The commercial lead-ins not only constitute almost half the lines devoted to the TV News broadcast skit, but also relate the consumption of advertised products such as breakfast food to the sexy appeal of a serial killer. Here is a perfect example of ambivalence in contemporary drama and its inevitable turn to subjectivity: *Coming Attractions* both performs television and contests television's valuation of the celebrity news item as commodity fetish, a critique which nevertheless reverberates back onto the play's own imaging illusions and ironic doubleness. The play "sells" its own images to demonstrate the selling of TV images. Or as Blau argues in a discussion about the equation of actors with commodities, in theater "there is . . . *no way of escaping the commodity form*" ("Ideology" 433; emphasis in original).

Coming Attractions, especially in scenes like the TV News broadcast skit, demonstrates that because the visual media deal in representation rather than "reality," the viewer doesn't actually desire the real thing but rather the proferred image. Consequently, an individual like Lonnie, in circulating as one more image in the performance of a television world, calls attention to the play world's "reality" as mediatized, a political position Raymond Williams critiques as technological determinism.[3] However, human agency does exist in this world, certainly for Manny, who clearly understands that actions, politics, and even criminal behavior are more often "created" than determined: "how many times I gotta tell you," he says to Lonnie, "it ain't news till some jerk of a writer invents it" (283).

Indeed, Manny's theater savvy enables him throughout the play to shape random actions into the kind of dramatic performance that appeals to the media culture, ultimately staging Lonnie's most spectacular stunt, the attempted shooting of Miss America, in front of TV cameras. Interestingly, though, because Manny's uses of theatricality ultimately occur in theater space, we are always self-reflexively returned to the ground of signs and the reproduction of images in the semiotic field of the play itself. *Coming Attractions* indicates that its televisual world relies on the same theatrical processes—signs, images, props, costumes, actors, voyeurism, desire—that are used to actualize the performance of a play (even one structured like television). At the same time, the play also shows how the very same theatrical processes are used to generate images and retail them to a variety of other cultural institutions, a practice that tends to deregulate territorial boundaries among media. (In fact, the term "theatricality," while having its origin in the playhouse, is now an interdisciplinary concept used in a number of discourses.)

Thus, in revealing an "economy" of image production and consumerism in the ground of the play itself, *Coming Attractions* does not pretend to stand apart from the culture it performs and contests. Indeed, the ironic position of the play shows theater participating in a postmodern world, and suggests that the humanist aesthetic of a better society achievable through the auspices of high culture has irretrievably declined. At least since Andy Warhol's multiple reproduction of celebrity faces, human desire has become intimately connected to fetishization. *Coming Attractions* does not pose as the elite, unsullied satirist of a media culture, for every critical comment it makes involves a subjective assessment as well.

Moreover, the subjective assessment occurs at the psychoanalytic level, which goes to the changing subjectivity of individu-

als in a media culture and, as I develop in Chapter 1, the subjectivity of drama itself. As the play indicates in its opening scene,
Lonnie wants to be watched by television, perhaps in the form of
Dan Rather or Geraldo Rivera. By virtue of being broadcasted he
more generally wishes to be seen by the other at large. By extension, *Coming Attractions* points to the sort of subjectivity offered
to viewers by television, performance, and a media culture generally.

Once Lonnie has been appropriated into television's visible
field, we are able to grasp how he, at first, begins to feel recognized, whole, identified by television and, through it, by an ador-
ing public. Acting out the TV viewer's frustrated desire to be on
television (witness how self-conscious spectators become at
baseball games when recognized by the camera), our populist
hero has managed to be seen by the other and, most importantly,
to see himself in some identity—serial killer. Significantly,
Mickey in Stone's film utters the line, "I'm a natural born
killer," precisely at the moment he is being televised live. In a
bizarre twist, violence becomes important social rather than antisocial behavior, for Lonnie and Mickey each believe that they
can perceive and locate themselves as an essentialist self with
respect to television (and its viewers) as other.

Yet *Coming Attractions* also indicates that because he has
switched on the gaze of television, Lonnie has also become the
image of a serial killer, a representation, a picture for broadcast,
fractured as a subject at the very moment of seeming coherence.
Indeed, at the instant he becomes the viewed, the serial killer identity cracks, making him unable to shoot his next victim. And as
television continues to pick him up, he crystallizes into the numerous icons of a media star—talk show guest, club singer, miniseries
actor. In short, Lonnie emerges from the process of constructing a
subjectivity as a quasi-subject by entering the circulation of
images always playing across the surface of the TV screen.

What Lonnie's situation ends up demonstrating is the inadequacy of an essentialist understanding of subjectivity for the
postmodern era. *Coming Attractions* implies that today just the
intent to discover a coherent, authentic self—whether as a TV-
viewing or theater-viewing subject—is a circular endeavor, for
intentionality has to stem from the belief in access to an authen-

tic self. In fact, the play disturbs the very notion of authenticity in art, which opens it up to the sort of criticism that sees its focus on television as an attack on the legitimacy and significance of theater. Yet the play is more accurately described as deconstructing a theatrical tradition that ignores theater's interconnections with other cultural institutions and its impact on social and political conditions. In *Coming Attractions*, theater is also shown to construct the individual and the world, which raises the question of whether an aesthetic of authenticity can be presented with any innocence in the late twentieth century.

In this way, the play not only places theater in a postmodern world, but also makes a significant point about the complexity of constructing subjectivity and what results from the process for both the TV and play viewer. *Coming Attractions* does not simply represent television; in attempting to perform and contest television, it deregulates the site of subjectivity in drama so that the problematic of the self, which has been in drama all along, is exposed to full view. The play is not only demonstrating Lonnie's desire; it is also uncovering how much the essentialist or humanist concepts of coherent selfhood and authenticity are no longer appropriate, having been ripped up by a media culture.

In terms of Lonnie's world, the method available for gaining selfhood exists as the individual's relation to television. Yet as the play shows, this process mediatizes the subject, a condition of the mediatized Imaginary I explore in Chapter 2. In terms of the audience's world, the play places our identity in a larger cultural project where we glimpse our own refracted faces flickering over the various "screens" of North America. *Coming Attractions* illustrates the point that, in a culture comprised of viewers, the desire to be seen and thus organized as a subject by an other operates in a constant exchange with the scopophilic demand to see and fetishize images. At the end of the second millennium, the desire of subjects becomes inseparable from the emergence of desired subjects, a condition of postmodern life that drives the world toward iconicity.

Coming Attractions immerses its audience in a media culture, a world particularly dominated by the influence of television. Yet as Philip Auslander suggests in *Presence and Resistance*, there is a place from which performance can resist a media culture even while operating within its terms (171). The ironic doubleness of *Coming Attractions* allows it to perform and contest television, to recognize its own situation in the postmodern era and still have something to say about what goes on in this "reality." Although the play was first performed at the start of the Reagan years, when even the American presidency became a theatrical event, it is clear that not much has changed as we proceed into the 2000s. The media still "pitch [their] tents," in Tally's words (Preface 275), around every serial killer (Jeffrey Dahmer) and notorious celebrity figure (O. J. Simpson) and involve all their viewers in the seduction, commodification, and circulation of images. One could even argue that Tally is representative of the way an individual can be seduced into a media culture, for he now writes for those twin media-scapes, television and Hollywood. (In fact, he won the Academy Award for Best Adapted Screenplay for *The Silence of the Lambs*.)

Certainly, the play illustrates just how problematic past notions of selfhood and authenticity are for the postmodern era. Yet perhaps the most valuable aspect of *Coming Attractions* lies in its acknowledgment of the contemporary drama's current significance. In ways that television is hampered in doing, drama can exercise its critical talent in exploring a media culture; at the same time, theater as a cultural institution can still be fully "in play" with the rest of the world. Nonetheless, plays that interrogate television and the media culture such as *Coming Attractions* always remind us that contemporary drama is very much an unfinished and ambivalent project, a "subject-in-progress," to borrow a term from Julia Kristeva.

Regardless of whether they were written in the 1960s or 1990s, these plays operate from a complex set of subject positions and often in strange combinations that run the gamut from contester, critiquer, satirist, parodist, and arbiter to celebrator, experimenter, and playful mediator. I would argue that postmodern drama most certainly has a future at the beginning of the twenty-first century and does not have to be subject to "an anxiety of contamination by its other" (vii), as Huyssen claims about modernism. Postmodern drama is not in danger of being swept aside, gobbled up, or infected by television.

If one were inclined to extend the theory of Jean Baudrillard to its logical conclusion, drama and its embodiment in the theatrical sign should not be possible in a world dominated by the screen, image, and code of television. Yet Baudrillard subverts his own message by filling up his writings with theatrical tropes, a sign that suggests the postmodern world may be modeled on dramatic codes as well as simulated.[4] And certainly the appearance of hundreds of new plays written and performed every year and numerous recent revivals of everything from *A Doll House* to *Chicago* implies that theater is escaping the dire fate expected by such apocalyptic visionaries because it already is in play with the "age of simulation," engaged in the deconstruction of binaries, fully involved in the postmodernist interrogation of essentialism, identity, genre, and medium. Recent plays such as Tally's are readily answering Bertolt Brecht's charge "to evolve an art fit for the times" (186), a postmodern drama for the media culture. That such an answer involves a continually vexed, agonistic, antagonistic negotiation of identity is the subject of this book.

Notes

1. See for instance: Paul Rudnick's *I Hate Hamlet*, William Gleason's *Happy Daze*, Jean-Claude van Itallie's *TV* in *America Hurrah*, Stuart Ross's *Forever Plaid*, Ronald Ribman's *Buck*, Megan Terry's *Brazil Fado*, Neil Simon's *Laughter on the 23rd Floor*, Lee Breuer's *Hajj: The Performance*.

2. The discussion of *Coming Attractions* revises an essay published in *Mosaic: A Journal for the Interdisciplinary Study of Literature* 28.4 (1995): 111-27. It is printed here with the permission of *Mosaic*.

3. In the 1970s Raymond Williams defined technological determinism as an ideology that attributes social change to the impact of new technologies. Technological determinists believe that "progress, in particular, is the history of these inventions, which 'created the modern world'" (7). Technological determinism continues to be a popular ideology, surfacing in some influential theories of the postmodern such as Jean Baudrillard's. Here, the image—often the TV image—is seen as determining the real.

4. In *America*, for instance, Baudrillard describes New York City as a stage play (22).

Works Cited

Auslander, Philip. *Presence and Resistance: Postmodernism and Cultural Politics in Contemporary American Performance*. Ann Arbor: U of Michigan P, 1992.

Bakhtin, M. M. *The Dialogic Imagination*. Ed. Michael Holquist. Trans. Caryl Emerson and Michael Holquist. Austin: U of Texas P, 1981.

Baudrillard, Jean. *America*. Trans. Chris Turner. London: Verso, 1988.

Birringer, Johannes. *Theatre, Theory, Postmodernism*. Bloomington: Indiana UP, 1993.

Blau, Herbert. *The Audience*. Baltimore: Johns Hopkins UP, 1990.

——. "Ideology, Performance, and the Illusions of Demystification." *Critical Theory and Performance*. Ed. Janelle G. Reinelt and Joseph R. Roach. Ann Arbor: U of Michigan P, 1992. 430-45.

Brecht, Bertolt. *Brecht on Theatre: The Development of an Aesthetic*. Ed. and trans. John Willett. New York: Hill & Wang, 1964.

Collins, Jim. "Postmodernism and Television." *Channels of Discourse, Reassembled: Television and Contemporary Criticism*. Ed. Robert C. Allen. Chapel Hill: U of North Carolina P, 1992. 327-53.

Douglas, Mary. *Purity and Danger: An Analysis of Concepts of Pollution and Taboo*. New York: Praeger, 1966.

Hallin, Daniel C. "We Keep America on Top of the World." *Watching Television*. Ed. Todd Gitlin. New York: Pantheon, 1986. 9-41.

Herman, Edward S., and Noam Chomsky. *Manufacturing Consent: The Political Economy of the Mass Media*. New York: Pantheon, 1988.

Hutcheon, Linda. *Splitting Images: Contemporary Canadian Ironies*. Toronto: Oxford UP, 1991.

Huyssen, Andreas. *After the Great Divide: Modernism, Mass Culture, Postmodernism*. Bloomington: Indiana UP, 1986.

Jameson, Fredric. *Postmodernism: or, The Cultural Logic of Late Capitalism*. Durham: Duke UP, 1991.

Kalem, T. E. "Fizz and Fury." Rev. of *Coming Attractions*, by Ted Tally, Jack Feldman, and Bruce Sussman. *Time* 15 Dec. 1980: 86.

Klaver, Elizabeth. "Postmodernism and the Intersection of Television and Contemporary Drama." *Journal of Popular Culture* 27.4 (1994): 69-80.

McLuhan, Marshall. *Essential McLuhan.* Ed. Eric McLuhan and Frank Zingrone. New York: Basic Books, 1995.

Natural Born Killers. Directed by Oliver Stone. Warner Bros., 1994.

Oliver, Edith. Rev. of *Coming Attractions* by Ted Tally, Jack Feldman, and Bruce Sussman. *New Yorker* 15 Dec. 1980: 80-82.

States, Bert O. "The Phenomenological Attitude." *Critical Theory and Performance.* Ed. Janelle G. Reinelt and Joseph R. Roach. Ann Arbor: U of Michigan P, 1992. 369-79.

Tally, Ted. Preface. *Coming Attractions.* By Ted Tally, Jack Feldman, and Bruce Sussman. *Plays from Playwrights Horizons.* New York: Broadway Play Publishing, 1987. 275.

Tally, Ted, Jack Feldman, and Bruce Sussman. *Coming Attractions.* *Plays from Playwrights Horizons.* New York: Broadway Play Publishing, 1987. 273-329.

Williams, Raymond. *Television: Technology and Cultural Form.* Hanover: Wesleyan UP, 1992.

Williams, Tennessee. *The Glass Menagerie.* New York: New Directions, 1970.

1

A QUESTION OF SUBJECTIVITY

The vast number and variety of subject positions—contester, satirist, celebrator, to name a few—that plays occupy with respect to television suggest that the identity of postmodern drama, rather than residing in some essentialist condition of ideological individualism, is in a continual state of flux. The very fact that drama "places" television in the position of object—the contested, the satirized, the celebrated—implies that questions of subjectivity are at issue, for the reciprocity of an object position is a necessary epistemology toward knowing the subject. Indeed, as pointed out in the Introduction, Andreas Huyssen argues this case with respect to the dependence of modernism on its other—mass culture (16)—and certainly for drama the very act of generating subject positions means circulating desire through some other. In a very real sense, theater pursues itself in the pursuit of the other, and while it undoubtedly looks to many "others"—film comes readily to mind—it clearly involves television in playing out this role. The purpose of this chapter, then, is to explore to what extent such subject positions are fundamentally correlated to the misrecognitions involved in masking the fissures of subjectivity, and how the other—television —is an absolute necessity for dramatic and theatrical self-scrutiny and performative identity in the media culture. In order to make this argument, I use the post-Lacanians Ernesto Laclau and Chantal Mouffe to connect the theory of subject positioning with Lacanian and Sartrian notions of subjectivity.

One of the most powerful theories of subjectivity is, of course, Jacques Lacan's. It has been particularly important to theories of the visual media, because it has to do with what happens in the field of the visible—the exchange of looks and glances, the operation of the gaze and the returned gaze, voyeurism and exhibitionism, the objectivity of the image, and so on. Lacan's theories of the mirror image and the gaze, described in *Ecrits* and *The Four Fundamental Concepts of Psychoanalysis* respectively, have been developed to describe functions of spectatorship by such theorists as Christian Metz for film, Barbara Freedman for theater, and John Ellis for television.

Very briefly, Lacan argues that subjectivity is initially organized in the Imaginary order as a function of an infantile "mirror stage," a phase that represents the moment when the subject, whose experience of the body so far has been disorganized and fragmented, recognizes in the mirror (or some other that plays the role of the mirror) the image of a whole, coherent, stable self, and happily absorbs it. All is not Edenic, though, as Lacan goes on to suggest. This impression of wholeness is a *méconnaisance,* or misrecognition, for the subject can never rid itself of the sense of fragmentation. The illusion of wholeness will always be haunted by a lack of completeness. At the time of entry into the Symbolic order, which Lacan correlates to the Oedipal stage and the acquisition of language, the *objet a* comes to represent what is missing, the lack that has been installed at the heart of subjectivity. Desire is what Lacan calls the effort by the subject throughout the course of his/her lifetime to overcome the sense of lack by pursuing the *objet a.*

In her discussion of Lacan's mirror stage, Julia Kristeva describes how the mirror image comes to be connected to the world at large: "the specular image is the 'prototype' for the 'world of objects.' Positing the imaged ego leads to the positing of the object" (100). Thus, the notion of a world of others begins to come into view. The functions of subjectivity Lacan theorized at the mirror stage enable him to proceed to what commentators such as Martin Jay have recognized as a move from the theory of the Imaginary to the theory of the gaze (Jay 367).

In this discussion of what happens to subjectivity in the field of the visible, the effect of the other and especially the gaze of the other becomes paramount. The other takes on such a foundational role for subjectivity for Lacan because its gaze as *objet a* represents what the subject desires, what the subject pursues to fill the lack occupying subjectivity. But like the illusion of wholeness posited at the mirror stage, the gaze is not fully attainable. The gaze cannot fill the lack, in part because it represents the lack and in part because it is imagined. Rather, the gaze serves its role for the subject in the circulation of desire, "symbolizing the central lack of desire" as Lacan writes (105), indeed reminding the subject that lack exists. Another way to put this is to say that the gaze is desirable, but that it is also lacking, and therefore not only cannot complete subjectivity, but also ruptures or subverts any illusion of complete or stable subjectivity that has been previously installed. This sort of gaze—the Lacanian gaze—does not proceed out of the subject, but rather is imagined by the subject as the returned gaze of the object.

Throughout the seminars on the gaze, Lacan is clearly influenced by phenomenology, especially the theories of Maurice Merleau-Ponty and Jean-Paul Sartre, which he engages extensively. In fact, Lacan refers to what he acknowledges to be a particularly brilliant section of Sartre's *Being and Nothingness,* and uses it to extend a discussion of how the other's gaze reorganizes the subject's world (84). Like Lacan, Sartre also theorizes subjectivity with respect to the other in what he calls the relation of the "For-itself" to the "For-others." He understands the For-itself as a subjectivity or consciousness that can never "be," a condition of Lacanian becoming that Kristeva characterizes as "a want-to-be [*manque à être*]" (101). Immediately noticeable is the similarity of the For-itself to Lacan's notion of subjectivity, because the For-itself also never attains wholeness or completeness, but rather remains in a constant, liminal state of becoming or deferral. Indeed, Jay rightly points out that Lacan and Sartre "both posited a desiring subject, whose primordial lack could never be filled either by internalizing the look of the other or by accepting the 'misrecognition' of the mirror" (347).

In Sartre's schemata, the other is fundamental to the structure of the For-itself, because the subject needs the other "to realize fully all the structures of [his/her] being" (303). This idea is very similar to M. M. Bakhtin's I-for-myself (the subject as it feels to its own consciousness), which is thoroughly dependent on the I-for-others (the subject as it appears to others) and the others-for-me (the others as they appear to me) (Holquist xxx; Bakhtin 37). While one has to take issue with his sense that these structures are fully realizable, Sartre's point is that certain complex reflections of the For-itself are dependent on the existence of the other, a relation to the other, and on "being-seen-by-the-other." Sartre gives the example of shame. A self-reflexive consciousness of shame only comes into play when the subject realizes an other has seen him/her do something shameful. Shame does not exist for the subject alone; shame is felt *"before somebody"* (302). Sartre writes that "the Other is the indispensable mediator between myself and me" (302); the other is that "somebody" who mediates the internal structures of subjectivity.

One of the most interesting innovations in Sartre's notion of the relation of the For-itself to the For-others is the recognition of the subjecthood of the other. In order for the subject to understand being-seen-by-the-other, the subject must view the other as a subject, for as Sartre claims only a subject has the capacity to operate a look. This also means that the subject must recognize its own objecthood, for there can be no subject-to-subject, nor indeed no object-to-object, relationship. This chiasma is what Sartre refers to as the subject's becoming a "being-as-object" to the other's becoming a "being-as-subject" (344-45).

The notion of the other's subjecthood gives rise to two additional, highly significant ideas. One is Sartre's understanding of spatiality, an understanding that translates to both theater and televisual space. A set of relations that concerns a subject, an other, and a gaze in the field of the visible must already involve spatiality, but in particular, and this is one of the ideas that intrigued Lacan, to Sartre the other's subjecthood reorders spatiality around itself. With the recognition of the other's subjecthood, the subject realizes that things in the world become oriented toward the other (343). All of this reordering still takes place within the space of the subject, of course, but now there is, according to Sartre, a "fixed sliding" of the universe, "a decentralization of the world which undermines the centralization which [the subject is] simultaneously effecting" (343). The subject as the center of his/her universe undergoes a swerve, and instead of a grouping of things toward the subject, there is now a fleeing away (342). Note how in the Bakhtinian discourse the subject becomes the object "me" in the expression "other-for-me."

Sartre's notion of the other's subjecthood as well as the consequent fixed sliding of the subject is one major piece Lacan uses to extend phenomenology to describe the decentering of the subject provoked by the Lacanian gaze. When the subject feels "under the Lacanian gaze," an epistemological impression of the split in subjectivity is provoked, which has the effect of not only decentering the subject—turning the subject into a being-as-object—but also reordering spatiality toward whatever is seen as generating the Lacanian gaze. I take this to be the point of Lacan's story of the sardine can. Contrary to the claim of Petit-Jean, clearly Lacan *is* being-seen-by-the-other ("it was looking at me, all the same"), and for a brief, uncomfortable moment undergoes a reordering of spatiality, finds things in his world, including his own subjecthood, grouping toward the sardine can (95).

Spatiality and its decentering effect is helpful in describing what occurs in performance, whether in the theater or television site, if we think of the play or television program in the position of the object and the audience or TV viewer occupying the position of the subject. Such a spatial field with its concomitant gazes outlines the basic voyeuristic contract. At times, though, where the voyeuristic subject position is expected, the audience or TV viewer can be forced to recognize the other's subjecthood through techniques like hyperconscious commentary or an invoking of the Lacanian gaze. For instance, plays and TV programs that break the illusion of realism by directly addressing the audience or viewer provoke momentarily a dis-ordering of spatiality around the subject. Plays that contain internal playlets (*Marat/Sade* for example) menace even more thoroughly the voyeuristic contract by aligning the theater audience with an on-stage audience, making them part of the performance, actually *looking* at them as part of the play semiotics. Indeed, according to Barbara Freedman, the Lacanian gaze is always already operating in theater space by the condition that "we are stared down by a look that challenges our own and reveals it as defined by another" (71).

TV studio audiences are placed in the same performative position: in fact, the presence of TV cameras and monitors profoundly invokes the Lacanian gaze and rattles the subject/object binary. I experienced such an unnerving in 1991 when I attended a taping of *The Tonight Show*. At one point, the television cameras were turned around to film the audience, broadcasting our images to millions of television viewers. The voyeur in her darkened recess was suddenly exposed to the brilliant, unforgiving light of television. In such a case, the subject quite literally becomes a being-as-object, finding herself and everything around her grouping toward the TV show's being-as-subject. The effect of this dis-ordering, whether in a TV studio or playhouse, is indeed a fixed sliding of the subject's universe, a discomfiting rupture in the subject's illusion of coherent and centered subjectivity.

The second important notion to which Sartre's understanding of the other's subjecthood gives rise is that subject/object and subject/other relations are highly unstable, variable, and vulnerable, a view that forecasts post-Lacanian theories of subject positioning. According to Hazel E. Barnes, Sartre's translator, the instability of subject and object underpins "the whole edifice of Sartrian love, hate, sadism, masochism, and even indifference," in fact all of the conflict and turmoil in the undercurrent of human relations (L). Any subject is always vulnerable to any other by virtue of the subject's immediate possibility of turning into a being-as-object. Indeed, here resides in the Sartrian condition of subject/object instability a significant contribution to the understanding of how flux and chiasma operate in subject positions and in theories of subject positioning, for it is quite apparent that subjects have reciprocal relations with the other (to desire/to be desired) and that these relations are vulnerable to rapid change.

Recently, theorists of subjectivity from feminists such as Judith Butler to the post-Lacanians have begun to recognize that the subject is not governed by any one essentialist or individualist notion of the self, but is realized within the possibilities of numerous and contingent subject positions. Although they put it in more ideological terms than Sartre, Laclau and Mouffe understand as well that any particular position of the subject generated at any moment in time is always open to change: "As every subject position is a discursive position, it partakes of the open character of every discourse" (115). Moreover, the modes of subjectivization—the generation of subject positions—according to Laclau and Mouffe is the way ideology acts as a misrecognition, attempting to "fill in" the lack or mask the decentered, fractured societal character of Lacanian subjectivity (see Laclau and Mouffe, 88n). Putting aside for now the question of ideology (which I take up more explicitly in Chapters 2 and 4), the post-Lacanians enable a link to be established between social, Marxist theory of the subject and Lacanian and Sartrian subjectivity. The post-Lacanian Anthony Elliott writes, "the interweaving of the imaginary and social reality arises when subjects come to recognize the *other person's subjectivity*" (192), a description very like Sartre's notion of a subject's recognition of the other's being-as-subject.

It is now possible to see that a subject position taken toward the other, because it is unstable, open to the possibility of chiasma and spatial reordering, is both a negotiation of the subject to the other and a misrecognition of subjectivity. In other words, the subject position produced out of a negotiation with the other is the misrecognition that covers over the fissures in subjectivity. This condition may be translated to the relation of drama and theater to television in the following way. Like the human subject, drama ought to be able to delineate subject positions by the object positions in which it places television. This claim certainly is valid in the larger cultural arena of discussions of television where agency is clearly operative: for instance, critics and scholars in drama studies, in attempting to define a position or demarcate a place for television, are actually generating subject positions for drama. A theater reviewer who castigates television for producing junk culture is inevitably generating a subject position for drama as the locus of elite culture. I want to argue that this manner of negotiating subject position is also valid in drama as a genre and its performance in the cultural institution of theater, specifically in the realm of postmodern plays and performances. Plays and performances, even though they are not carbon-based, exhibit many of the characteristics associated with the human subject: the Lacanian orders of the Imaginary, Symbolic, and Real; a Butlerian mode of performative and identifying acts; a non-essentialist, fractured subjectivity; a hyperconsciousness; the ability to make commentary; even a sort of generic agency. And without question, plays and performances that incorporate televisual discourse are looking to television to perform a number of the functions of the other, all of which have to do fundamentally with the misrecognitions and subjectivity of drama and theater.

Of course, one may readily point out that if television is indeed the other of drama, what did drama do before television? My contention is not that television is the only other, but a particularly important, historically contextualized other among a range of others to which drama and theater are ineluctably tied. The theoretical notion popular in the Renaissance of drama "holding up a mirror to nature" is another way of saying that drama is other to nature, here the image of the mirror. Or to turn it around, as Shakespeare does in lines like "All the world's a stage" (*As You Like It,* II.vii.139), the world holds up the mirror, thus operating as other to drama.

The play *Noises Off* by Michael Frayn is a very good example of how television, even when appearing in the background of a play, may be positioned as an object in order to negotiate subject positions for the play and for theater itself. To begin with, *Noises Off,* a parody of British bedroom-farce, is already hyperconscious about performance, being about a theater group putting on a play. More specifically, it is based on the self-reflexive conceit of "going around behind the scene," exposing what goes on in the rehearsal of a play, what goes on backstage during performance, and how performance is thus affected. *Noises Off* includes a fictitious program that details the imaginary particulars of a farcical comedy entitled "Nothing On." Act 1 presents "Nothing On" in rehearsal and introduces the undercurrent of love affairs, petty rivalries, and jealousies among the cast. Act 2 turns the set around, enabling the audience to witness the shenanigans going on backstage during a performance and to glimpse through the doors and windows of the backdrop how much "Nothing On" is being disrupted as a consequence. Act 3 returns the set to its original position. Now the audience is treated to what "Nothing On" has become after three months of in-fighting, a performance in hilarious disarray.

The set of "Nothing On" is the living room of an aristocratic English family, "a place where the discerning theatre-goer will feel instantly at home" (1). In the production I attended, a television set was placed in the middle of the stage, its back to the audience and facing upstage. As part of the semiotic language of the play, the television set has several simple, but important, functions: as an icon it helps locate the time period of the play (the set is "fully equipped with every aid to modern living" [1]), for without an item belonging so definitively to the latter half of the twentieth century, *Noises Off* could occur at a much earlier date; it also acts as referent to several diegetic remarks made by the characters ("it's the royal" [see 2, 8, 9], "it's the colour" [9], "it's black-and-white at home" [9]), and provides the excuse for Mrs. Clackett's presence.

Of greater interest, though, is how the inclusion of the television set operates on the subject positions generated by the play. On the one hand, by turning the television screen away from the audience, *Noises Off* makes visible only the backside of the television set, producing a highly negative trope which positions television as an object of jeer. It is the technological equivalent of the numerous pratfalls in the play where a human backside is exposed, a standard farcical prank. And by "exposing" television as an artistic prank, *Noises Off* places television in the object position of a lesser art form, scrutinized as little more than the "backside" of theatrical performance. Moreover, since the television set is not turned on, since its programs are not viewable, since indeed it has "nothing on," the play implies that theater is a more satisfying medium. Given the choice, would not an audience rather watch a play than a television show? And, to be sure, this play being so much about theater undoubtedly is best seen in theater space than in any other medium (even though a film version does exist).

In this interpretation, *Noises Off* positions television in such a way that a subject position for the play is returned. An epistemological negotiation occurs that allows the play and its dramatic embodiment to "know" itself, in this particular case as satirizer, scrutinizer, high culture. In fact, as *Noises Off* demonstrates, when plays incorporate television or televisual discourse, even in the most tangential manner, television never just sits there as an innocent bystander, an empty property, empty set of references, empty structure, indeed empty sign, although more often than not it is read in just this way. In my library copy of *The Sunshine Boys,* Neil Simon's 1972 play about the influence of vaudeville theater on early television comedy, someone who used the book as a production copy pencilled out the entire opening scene of Willie's dialogue with his television set. My guess is that the reader did not notice how important this cyborgian relationship is to the humor, the irony, or the meanings of the play, even though the scene is quite easy to stage.

In fact, when it appears in a play, television operates an enormous set of discourses relating to its role as other and as being-as-subject to theater. Just as it does in our living rooms, television on stage offers all sorts of functions associated with the other—images that mirror back an illusion of complete subjectivity, repeating gaps of reflective (b)lack, desires that cannot come to fruition, a continual lure of visual and aural voyeurism. Indeed, the ghostly network logos—the CBS eye or ABC's circle—written over the lower right corner of the television screen are very similar to the skull Lacan sees in Holbein's *Ambassadors,* functions of the gaze as *objet a,* Lacanian *ocelli* that appear to look back at the viewer. Moreover, the circulation of images and the complex of looking structures in the field of the visible suggest that television repeatedly attempts and ultimately fails to "fill in" a fantasy of complete subjectivity not only for the TV viewer but for the subjectivity of drama and theater as well.

Surprisingly, the misrecognitions offered by the televisual discourse in a play are demonstrated in Tennessee Williams's *Cat on a Hot Tin Roof.* I say surprisingly, not only because *Cat* is an early play to be dealing with television and is not considered postmodernist, but also because drama scholars and directors have not generally noticed that a television set is included in the play's call for a combination console of stereo, TV, and liquor cabinet (xiii-xiv). Nevertheless, as in *Noises Off* the television set provides a number of important semiotic functions in *Cat,* from connoting themes of escapism and existential crisis to ideological messages of normality to the illusions of subject position. In the design notes, Williams links the console to the play's theme of mystification, calling it a "little shrine" to the illusions of the characters, a repository for the fantasies of us all (xiv).

A recent production (1999) in Carbondale, Illinois, is one of the few performances of *Cat* I have found that not only includes the television set but actually turns it on, here to the broadcast of a baseball game.[1] The audience clearly hears the play-by-play announcer say, "Here's the pitch," which produces a nice reminder of Brick's failure as a sports announcer; perhaps more importantly, it offers a reflective image to Brick that is much more coherent than the source, with his fractured leg and spirit. The televisual other produces a fantasy of heterosexual "manliness," which may be read as an ideological attempt to mask a certain turbulence in Brick's subjectivity—to impose a subject position of "normality"—but which undoubtedly opens as many fissures as it attempts to close. Indeed, Judith Butler makes the point that "one way in which [the] system of compulsory heterosexuality is reproduced and concealed is through the cultivation of bodies into discrete sexes with 'natural' appearances and 'natural' heterosexual dispositions" (275). And television has always been one of the system's primary conduits.

The ambivalence of Brick's sexual identity, which remains a mystery throughout the play, provides the greatest clue that issues of subjectivity in drama and theater are at stake. To some critics such as David Savran, Brick is quite clearly identified as homosexual. But the semiotic codes of *Cat* never seem to come down squarely on this subject position, primarily because it is the illusion of heterosexuality that is always being mirrored, and rather than producing a sexual identity for Brick, this particular televisual image—this mask—performs a radical failure in negotiation. Regardless of whether Brick can sustain the illusion of "normal" sexuality, his subjectivity remains incoherent and ultimately unresolvable. And, to be sure, what makes *Cat* such a great play is that all of this turbulence in subjectivity is plainly observable, observable as a dramatic and generic problematic as well as a human one. The play itself undergoes a rupture in its sheen of coherence, allowing a glimpse into the fissures in the drama of the time, fissures that are also the topics of the play: not just homosexuality, but also alcoholism, cancer, and troubled marriage. *Cat* demonstrates that the fantasy of "normality" exuding from television fails to fill in at the level of the play's subjectivity as well, which has given rise to a number of critical problematics not the least of which is identity: is *Cat* a gay play?

Perhaps it is because television is in our homes so often playing the role of other and especially generating the Lacanian "lack of desire" that televisual discourse in a play becomes mes-merizing, so compelling that it cannot help but attract attention. No matter what it does on stage—from simply offering the back-side of the TV set to the voice of an announcer, from the blank-ness of a TV screen to the patter of flickering lights, from the unswerving gaze of a camera to a full-scale imagistic assault—television is definitely distracting, making everything turn toward it. (In the Carbondale production of *Cat* the male characters at one point all become distracted by the ball game on television.) And when everything does turn toward television, when things in the playworld group toward it, Sartre's notion of a change in spa-tiality and its effects on subjectivity ultimately come into play.

In the sort of theater site where plays are performing televi-sion, the televisual discourse is literally acting on the play and on things in the play, becoming a being-as-subject to the play. Indeed, the very process of negotiating subject positions indi-cates that a play is obliged to recognize the subjecthood of some other—here television—and place itself before the gaze "of somebody." This epistemological paradigm is complicated by the fact that subject positions, as suggested above in the Sartrian and post-Lacanian systems, are the illusions of misrecognition, including the misrecognition of stability. As it is for any subject, a state of enormous flux makes a play vulnerable to the poten-tiality of chiasma, of becoming a being-as-object to the other. Of course, this highly variable situation is a necessary consequence of the desire to pursue the *object a,* to "fill in" the lack in subjec-tivity. In order to realize the structures of its being, as Sartre puts it (303), a play would have to understand itself as being-seen-by-the-other and, thus, it would have to recognize that television has a subjecthood. All of this ends up propelling the play's world toward the televisual discourse.

To return to *The Sunshine Boys* as an example, the opening scene shows everything, especially the elderly vaudeville actor, turning toward television. Companion, conversant, and friend, television is the only other in a lonely life, offering images of a fuller, more vibrant subjectivity even if, ironically, in the two-dimensionality of an afternoon soap opera. Once the television set comes unplugged at the end of this scene, television's role as other and its effects on spatiality would appear to be over. On the contrary, the opening scene actually forecasts the rest of the play, which revolves around the notion of reuniting a two-man comedy team for a television special on the history of comedy. Act 2, for instance, takes place in a television studio where the comedy bit is being rehearsed. Indeed, it becomes clearer as the play progresses that not just the story or things in the playworld are fleeing toward television, but pressing epistemological questions about theater are being oriented in the same way, questions about its role, its influence on television, and its viability in the media culture. Of course, like the situation of the human subject, all of this "fleeing" takes place within theater space and within the space of the play, where dramatic functions always form the "ground." But now the ground has become a highly liminal topography, where in the course of a play's attempt to position itself, something happens.

What happens is a decentralization of subjectivity, or as Sartre might put it, the undermining of the centralization of the play in the course of television looking back. A deconstruction in knowledge about the subject occurs, perhaps most obviously evidenced in the unsettling of subject position to object. If, for instance, a play has appeared to negotiate the stance of satirist, a closer examination would undoubtedly reveal that such a position is highly unstable. While *The Sunshine Boys* may appear initially to ridicule television as a pathetic excuse for an other, once the searching gaze of television becomes felt the subject position of the play becomes less coherent. In fact, only the illusion of a stable subject position is ever really generated, very like the illusion of wholeness and stability offered by the misrecognition of the mirror image, which is merely covering over a highly fragmented condition. What such a decentralization ultimately does, then, is "remind" the play and its performance of the fractures in subjectivity, which of course only prompts the theatrical discourse to continue playing out its pursuit. In fact, those subject positions taken by drama toward television are correlated to the fractures in its subjectivity, and behave something like the give-and-go of game pieces across a board game of desire.

The notion of a decentralization of subjectivity helps explain what happens in the second and third acts of *Noises Off,* especially the disruptive nature of the third act, which displays the fissures always riding under the surface of theater's illusions. Besides the high culture stance, the placement of the television set in this play produces an additional, more complex subject position. In this interpretation, the backside of the television set represents the play's conceit of "going around behind" instead of just presenting the front. And *Noises Off* is indeed about uncovering, about delving into some "truths" hidden behind the scenes. The play pursues the onstage television apparatus as an other, a somebody whose "blank eye" will establish this particular subject position. But as one would expect, in order to involve the televisual discourse in this way the play has to confer subjecthood on television, not simply object status, because to paraphrase Sartre if the other is necessarily part of the looking complex in the field of the visible, the other must operate its gaze from the position of subjecthood. Television is not simply an other, a backside to be "exposed," but an other which is very much involved in doing the "exposing." As a being-as-subject, television becomes part of the scrutinizing project of the play in which theater undergoes the chiasma of a subject to a being-as-object. This suggests that theater must also have a "backside" of some sort that can be presented to view.

Indeed, presenting the backside of theater is what the play proposes to do in the second act by turning the set around so that the audience watches the backstage behaviors that construct, or in this case also subvert, the illusions of performance. But in the process of turning the set around, the television set is also turned around, so that now its screen faces the audience even though it is not actually visible to the eye. Interestingly, what was once the backside has now become the "front-side," so that just at the moment when the play should be most behind, the other no longer reflects this subject position. It offers instead a trope of frontality, suggesting that *Noises Off* never really does go behind the scenes.

What the television set now demonstrates is that the play just goes to another front, to showing another scene, which is backstage made frontal. Of course, this is the classic phenomenological problematic: everything is indeed always frontal. There is no such thing, really, as the "backside," or at least it is not available to the visible field of ordinary human beings, and as Bert O. States remarks, theater is one place where this "frontality of experience" is clearly demonstrated (371). The television apparatus in *Noises Off* still operates as a being-as-subject, but what it ultimately exposes is the illusion of the play's conceit.

It indicates that when the play attempts to uncover the illusory apparatus of performance, it does so by constructing an illusion, and the image that television as other reflects shows how this construction is achieved. However, once the phenomenological problematic of "going around behind" is made manifest and the play returns to its front side (act 3), the actual instability of its subject position(s) and lack of coherent subjectivity become apparent. When the logic of its placement of the televisual discourse is followed through in act 3, *Noises Off* suggests that the performance, in scrutinizing television, undergoes a chiasma to self-scrutiny, the being-as-object status that is, to subjectivity, an epistemological imperative. Drama is shown to have ruptures that lie beneath the sheen of misrecognition: none of its subject positions can be said to rest on "firm ground." What is so compelling about the televisual discourse in *Noises Off* is that even though it fails to fill in the fantasy of "going behind," television nevertheless allows a glimpse into the play's churning subjectivity by deconstructing the mask of the theatrical image.

Noises Off and *Cat* demonstrate that, even if it is in the background of a play, televisual discourse can be seen as having an enormous impact on the way a play as well as theater positions and knows itself as subject. Certainly, *The Quintessential Image* by Jane Chambers and *Voice of the Machine* by Warner Blake go much further in taking up the issue of subjectivity by placing television in the foreground and inviting the new medium to interrogate explicitly the epistemological parameters of knowing the "self" of drama and theater. Clearly postmodernist, both plays illustrate the theoretical point that all scrutiny of the other comes back to the subject as self-scrutiny and that all such commentary ultimately negotiates identity.

As I have argued, the placing of television as object in a play enables for the play and its performance a negotiation of subject position as well as a demonstration of the lack in subjectivity to occur. In a field that is as oriented to the visible as theater, more precisely this process relies on the looking functions associated with a sort of generic "eye" that theater uses for scrutinizing the objecthood of the other, in this case television. Indeed, the phenomenological problematic identified above in *Noises Off* is already an indication of the existence of this eye and some of its functions of scrutiny, functions that are much more complex than simply locating the objecthood of television and thus the subject position of drama. Inevitably, this eye is used to pursue the *objet a* in the televisual gaze.

As demonstrated in Lacan's story of the sardine can, the circulation of desire in the field of the visible means that theater must recognize on some level that it is being-seen, at the very least at the level of light (95). Sartre and the post-Lacanians would go even further, insisting that the felt gaze of the other requires theater not only to see with its own eye but to recognize the eye of television. Certainly, in some plays such as *Q Image,* television's eye—its being-as-subject—is not only rendered explicit but veritably privileged. The desire of the gaze as part of knowing subjecthood operates as a way for the play to look at itself, so that the gaze comes back as a form of self-reflection or self-scrutiny of theater. However, as I will demonstrate, this process in itself raises serious epistemological problematics regarding the status of what does come back and the eye that returns it.

Q Image not only puts television precisely in the foreground—the play is set in a television taping studio—but also takes a much more positive attitude toward it than *Noises Off.* Contrary to Frayn's play, there does not appear to be a negative tropological discourse directed at television at all in *Q Image.* Television is taken seriously as an other with all of the necessary operations designated for that particular position. For instance, television is always "live"; the TV monitors are always on, generating looking functions not only as the source of light, but more importantly as the light of a scrutinizing eye. The play rests on the recognition that television is an other with a subjecthood, with the ability to engage in the visible field and to alter the spatiality of the play-world. Television is figured as a scrutinizer, a seer, even a "truth-sayer."

Q Image is the last play by Jane Chambers, and premiered in 1985 two years after her death. She is best known for her 1980 play *Last Summer at Bluefish Cove,* which was one of the first plays to present a non-pathological view of lesbianism. Interestingly, in her youth Chambers wrote, hosted, and acted in television shows before she became a serious playwright for the theater (Dean 3); so, in a sense, as her last play *Q Image* completes the circle. From the opening scene onward, *Q Image* operates from the understanding that the televisual and theatrical image is a pose, a misrecognition whose apparent coherence does not correspond to the turbulent nature of subjectivity. Moreover, the play expects the televisual discourse as well as the dramatic to participate in the project of deconstructing this pose.

Q Image opens on a television taping studio, where PBS-style television host Margaret Foy is about to interview before a live studio audience (played by the theater audience) award-winning photographer Lacey Lanier. Three television monitors are placed on the stage facing Margaret and Lacey, which present to them what the cameras are recording and enable them to see and respond to their own televisual images. In fact, the women are engaged in dialogue with their televisual selves, with recognizing and responding to the split generated by televisual mediation, between "myself and me," as Sartre would put it. *Q Image* examines the way human subjects are driven by the desire to pursue the *objet a* in the image of the other. The play depicts the subject's hope that by being-seen-by-the-other the lack will be filled and subjectivity experienced as complete and coherent. This psychological narrative is presented in the history of Lacey's career as a photographer.

Rather than setting out to capture in photographs the major events of the twentieth century, as everyone assumes, Lacey describes how she was always attempting to take a picture of one Belinda Adams, the unrequited love of Lacey's life. For instance, according to the stage directions the first photo that Lacey took portrays an American World War I soldier eating a piece of pie while disembarking from a train into the arms of a hometown crowd (10-11). It turns out that Lacey was actually trying to photograph Belinda, who appears only as "*a blurred image*" in the background of the scene (11).

The object of desire, personified as Belinda, is never in focus, as Lacey discovers, and in fact the effort throughout her career to bring it into focus always ends up producing some "other" image that takes on meanings of its own. The "other"—the cultural history of America—that actually emerges in the photos cannot accurately reflect Lacey's subjectivity, in part because it rejects her sexual identity and in part because it attempts to fill in the fissures in her subjectivity with those same ideological standards of normality apparent in *Cat*. (Interestingly, because normality is enforced by Lacey's mother, the Symbolic order is figured as a Law of the "[M]other.") Lacey says, "I spent my whole life taking pictures of Belinda, trying to hold her still, to make her look back at me and see me" (17). But it is not until she is famous that Lacey finally does get Belinda to look back. And what she discovers in that gaze is the inadequacy of the image, the subjecthood of the other, and the vulnerability of her own subject position. She sees hate (17).

The "piece of mirror" (10) that Lacey used to make her first camera and her first blurred image can never reflect an other who could adequately mask the fractures in her subjectivity. The play works to undo the coherence of images of the subject as represented by the photos and to demonstrate that the image is a mask for the subject. Of course, all of this exposure is taking place in the television studio, under the eye of the television camera and reflected on the monitors. The play looks to the televisual eye as a means for uncovering the "truth" about the image, for deconstructing one sort of image and for returning knowledge of a purer, indeed more *quintessential,* image of the subject.

As the play nears its conclusion, Lacey drops enough dangerous hints to come close to "outing" Margaret, and implies that Margaret should take a good look at her own pursuit of the image. Instead of chasing after the other, Lacey says, "You got to take a picture of yourself and get to love it" (18). The play suggests that by invoking the order of the Lacanian Imaginary the subject can construct a purer image of the self than the images imposed by the other's standards of normality. The play ends with Margaret alone in the studio, watching her picture on the television monitor and apparently coming to terms with the truth of her own sexual identity.

Thus, in admitting the subjecthood of television, *Q Image* suggests that the televisual discourse can perform the role of truth-sayer not only by exposing the truth but also by offering the truth. But, of course, this claim generates a significant epistemological problematic. Even as it demonstrates that images of gender are open to re-construction, as lesbian theorists such as Kate Davy and Sue-Ellen Case argue, the play comes close to positing an essentialist episteme: there is a true image of the self as *objet a* that can be captured; truth is available; and there is a transcendental signifier, a quintessential image, to point the way.[2] However, the status of this "televisual" essentialism is itself undercut by the play in three ways.

First of all, Margaret cannot simply find the truth by looking at her televisual image, for the televisual image is still a pose, perhaps a more coherent one, but a pose nevertheless that ultimately cannot fill in the fractures in subjectivity. Indeed, Margaret makes a telling pun that reveals the semiotic foundation of televisual discourse in which truth and meaning—*the objet a*—are always indefinitely deferred: in response to Lacey's use of a curse word, Margaret says, "This is television, Lacey. We have *to watch our language*" (9; emphasis added).

Second, the idea of loving one's own image brings to mind the way Freud linked homosexuality with narcissism. In "Leonardo da Vinci and a Memory of His Childhood," Freud theorized that the male homosexual, in desiring other men, is in actuality desiring the image of himself. The homosexual has "slip[ped] back to auto-erotism" (463). Although *Q Image* is dealing with gay women rather than gay men, there still lingers in Lacey's advice to Margaret the taint of pathology when this connection to Freud is made. This little psychological blot, surprising to find in a playwright so committed to portraying positive models of gay people, problematizes the purity of the televisual image.

Third, there will be editing. Margaret reminds us several times that the interview will "be cut and edited" (7). There is a good possibility that the "truth," even if it were available, would never make it out of the television studio. Apart from the personal pressures Margaret must feel, there are corporate and ideological pressures coming from television itself that will inevitably rewrite what has been exposed to the camera. The subject position taken by the play of viewing television as a truth-sayer becomes unstable once we realize that even the "quintessential image" is open to negotiation long before it is broadcast. Television may have the function of a public discourse, but not of a gospel.

If television cannot really be a truth-sayer, then what about drama in this subject position? After all, *Q Image* takes place in theater space. Even if the "truth" will never be broadcast by television, has not the theater audience just witnessed it? Although this is a tempting reading, it is sabotaged by the semiotic and performative foundation of the play itself. Dramatic discourse has all of the epistemological problematics discussed above with respect to television regarding the availability of truth and the *objet a*. In playing the studio audience, the theater audience has already arrived at a role within the parameters of *Q Image,* and has already negotiated an identity, to recast Judith Butler, through a series of performative acts (270).

According to performative theory, the subjectivity of the audience is as theatrical as any of the subjectivities presented on the stage, and thus precludes an essentialist model of the self as "truth-receiver" as much as it precludes one of truth-sayer. Furthermore, theater as a cultural institution is in the same position as the characters with respect to the televisual image. The televisual image is generating a more coherent picture of subjectivity than theater can manifest. In fact, the subject position of truth-sayer reflected in the televisual eye is far too coherent for theater, as well as television, to bear.

Thus, because theater is shown to be as imagistic as television, *Q Image* manages to create a loop in which the dramatic images and the televisual images look back at each other endlessly as if they were circulating through two reflective surfaces, an emblem of ironic self-scrutiny if ever there was one. This pursuit of misrecognition, rather than the "truth" of identity, is what the television monitors have always signified in the play, just as Lacey's photographs have. *Q Image* presents a narrative of the subjectivity of drama at the level of Lacanian desire or Sartrian becoming, a shifting, intensely volatile place—a performative place—that underlies the complex of functions of the subject.

All of the plays under discussion in this chapter point toward the notion that the unstable, variable subjectivity of drama and theater does outline a place of sorts, or at least the tropology of place. This is because the Imaginary and Symbolic orders limit the subject to imagining subjectivity only in physical contours, most often in the concrete terms of language, space, and image. The Lacanian mirror stage, for example, may be understood as the crucial moment when the (in)coherent subject is established as something that can and cannot occupy two places at once, something that can and cannot be inside and outside the mirror image. Freud figured subjectivity as physical shape, locating the unconscious in something like a cellar beneath the conscious mind. As well, Sartre's theory of spatiality and the chiasmic relationship of being-as-subject to being-as-object involves an articulation of three-dimensionality, perhaps best pictured as the way physicists imagine objects bending the profile of space. In this way, identity and the splitting of the subject come about as a physical and cultural articulation of the discourses used to draw the outlines of place. Certainly, for drama, the notions of subjectivity and place go hand-in-hand; after all, plays are physical entities of language, body, image, and performance, and the idea of theater connotes performance, site, and cultural institution—all the ontological concreteness of the dramatic signifier in a semiotic architecture.

Indeed, one of the most interesting theoretical returns is what happens to the place of theater's subjectivity when drama performs television. Such plays end up supporting the theory that the outlining of place must also be a misrecognition, a subject position that engages in the prospect of masking the disorganized nature of subjectivity. Of course, drama studies has often endeavored to draw a definite line between television and theater, embodying the cultural distinction of having either "a proper place" or being "out-of-place." The Wooster Group's *Route 1 & 9 (The Last Act),* for instance, was initially criticized for employing TV monitors on stage, as if theater were "no place" for television (LeCompte 231-32).

The tropology of "knowing one's place" describes to Marshall McLuhan the organization of epistemology from the sixteenth century onward as being based on the orderly arrangement of the printer's type, which designates "a place for everything and everything in its place" (285). Certainly, our culture at least to the advent of postmodernism associates physical locales with performances recognized as site specific: respectively, theater and television find their places in a public building or in the private home where they literally take, or "possess," place. But some plays like Blake's *Voice of the Machine* deliberately shred the boundaries of place and demonstrate the unsteadiness—the misrecognition—of such demarcations. *Voice* is a highly deconstructive play that like *Q Image* places television in the foreground, engaging it as an other in a similar project of uncovering the subjectivity of drama and theater.

The theater site of *Voice* is comprised of a small proscenium-arch stage at one end of a long conference table, around which sits an audience of twelve. The rest of the audience sits farther back. Opera glasses hang from scaffolding in front of each spectator. The third and final play in the *Soup Talks Trilogy*, *Voice* concludes the story of what happened to the last symphony orchestra, which went down in a plane crash over the Arctic. It was staged during the summer of 1996 at Newmark's Second Floor Gallery in Seattle, Washington.

When it is first shown to the audience, the television set is situated inside the proscenium stage. On the one hand, this placement may signify, as in *Noises Off,* that television is dominated by theater, dependent on theater and on the theatrical arts for its very being. Of course, because theater is in the position of subject, it must surround the televisual discourse, forming the frame and the physical and aesthetic ground, even though as Sartre points out, the subject—in this case, theater—may find its "self" undergoing a fixed sliding. On the other hand, such a careful act of placing television in *Voice* is complicated by the fact that the proscenium stage is itself placed inside a theater which is placed inside an art gallery. Indeed, at the ending of the play, the narrator invites the audience to look over "the installation." *Voice* produces a series of nested places which undoes the notion of place as a fixed structure with fixed boundaries, and offers instead the fluidity of *différance*—the trope of the *mise en abyme*. Moreover, the project of deconstructing place is enhanced by the television screen, which returns the image of a child with a television set in his background which is playing the same image and so on, *ad infinitum*. Therefore, the placement of televisual discourse inside the proscenium stage may also signify the full incorporation of television into drama with the aim of deconstructing not so much the image, as in *Q Image,* but the misrecognition of the theater site itself.

Place as misrecognition is further developed when the television set, at one point, rises above the top of the proscenium arch. Television literally escapes the physical boundary, and gets "out of place" in every sense of the trope. Is television now in the "subject position" of dominating theater? This would constitute a chiasmic reversal in the notion of television's domination by theater, and a demand that television be viewed as a "being" in its own right, certainly as a Sartrian being-as-subject. And finally, the demarcation of place is most radically undone by the story of the play's genesis. The narrator describes how he got the idea for *Voice* from *I Led Three Lives,* a 1950s television show about a man who posed as ordinary citizen by day and reported to the FBI from his attic by night. Now, the machine-that-sent-the-voice on *I Led Three Lives* has been reconfigured as the "voice of the machine." Interestingly, the originating impulse— the equivalent to the other of the Imaginary order—turns out to be television rather than drama.

What *Voice* further exemplifies is the notion that, like the human subject, the subjectivity of drama is continually bearing and circulating the image of the other. Through the process of filling in, the Imaginary order not only "originates" the coherence of the subject, but is always already re-originating it, re-circulating the other through the subject. Bearing the imprint of the other is a necessary function of misrecognition, and has to do with the subject's locating of him/herself as a being-as-object in spatiality. Certainly, as Christian Metz and others have theorized for film, the subjectifying process involves suturing the viewer to the cinematic other, a process that not only rearticulates the mirror stage but absorbs the other into the subject. For plays in performance, television as other becomes imprinted as Sartre's "indispensable mediator," allowing theater to circulate gazes in the field of the visible, to sustain scrutiny and the chiasma of self-scrutiny, to position itself in the spatiality of the media culture.

Even plays that do not specifically incorporate televisual discourse may bear at their very heart the imprint of television. Philip Auslander in "Liveness: Performance and the Anxiety of

Simulation" describes the way in which much of the contemporary theater, as well as other live performance genres, is indeed occupied by other media, "incorporat[ing] mediatization such that the live event itself is a product of reproductive technologies" (197). He observes that many Broadway productions, for example, are written and performed "camera-ready" for later broadcast on cable television (200). Of course, there is a cultural economy at work here as well as powerful marketplace forces. But I would also suggest that a fundamental reason this sort of mediatized performance is occurring more and more often is because postmodern drama is specifically attempting to negotiate subject positions with respect to the other media, and at the level of subjectivity the other is an ontological necessity for constructing these misrecognitions. As happens to the human subject, drama in its relationship to the other inevitably will be marked with the image of the other. The generation of a sense of coherent subjectivity, which all other negotiations of subject position, place, and identity articulate, simply has to include a debt to the other.

Voice puts a specific emphasis on the functions of the visible field in order to uncover this debt to the other, here the necessity of television to drama. The opera glasses, of course, not only magnify the visual acuity of the audience, but also draw attention to and magnify the importance of the act of seeing. Moreover, the play magnifies the notion of seeing others and being-seen-by-others by placing, late in the performance, a large semi-reflective screen in front of the proscenium stage. It is still possible to see the proscenium stage and the television set through the screen, but now one can also see the reflection of other audience members in the screen, although it is tilted in such a way that one does not see one's own reflection.

In this way, the play expresses how much subjectivity, knowledge of the self, and the positioning of the subject are dependent on circulating looking functions through the other. The play is figuring forth Lacan's notion that epistemologically "seeing" one's self means that seeing can only be generated by undergoing a swerve into and through the gaze of some other. To Lacan, the commonsensical idea of *"seeing oneself seeing oneself*—represents mere sleight of hand" (74); it is an illusion of consciousness (82). In seeing the other in *Voice,* the audience member not only understands that he/she is being seen-by-the-other, but also misrecognizes in the reflective screen a coherent image of his/her subjectivity and a coherent place in the theater site. Out of this image, he/she is able to formulate the subject as a subject among others, "to recognize *the other person's subjectivity*" as Elliott puts it, to negotiate place as misrecognition and subject position with respect to the rest of the audience and to the play and theater experience.

These processes of subjectivity at work in the audience member parallel the processes of subjectivity at work in postmodern drama and theater, and show how the act of scrutiny is returned as a self-scrutiny. *Voice* demonstrates that television, in acting as that slightly tilted screen, reflects images back to drama and to theater as a cultural institution that provide a way of self-looking, a way of attaining a sense of coherent subjectivity, a place and a variety of subject positions, however misrecognized. As Axel Honneth writes, "every individual [read play] is dependent on the possibility of constant reassurance by the Other" (189): plays need a reciprocal relationship to some other in order to look at themselves, know themselves, and thereby to formulate identity, which they ironically gain by admitting to both the objecthood *and* subjecthood of the other. Television becomes "the subject" of the mirror, the Bakhtinian other-for-me needed by the theater "self." To be sure, a play like *Voice* exemplifies how much drama is indebted to such an other, indeed how necessary such an other is to its internal and social structures of subjectivity and to its epistemological negotiation of identity as play, place, and cultural institution.

Of course, all of this discussion points to the ways postmodern drama and theater negotiate a place in the media culture, for it is only by recognizing and engaging the *other* media that performative genres and cultural institutions can situate themselves within a contemporary world. The idea that drama and theater can be treated as a closed system, held distinct from the media culture, could not be further from reality, for as Laclau and Mouffe argue, "all identity is relational" (113). Certainly, as Jeffrey Nealon points out, identity is not what one *has,* but "is, rather," in Levinas's words, "the 'event of the identification' that

I *am*" (59). And the fact that two and more media are at play in this "event" makes the relational nature of identity highly complex, for numerous discourses are involved, each replete with images, signs, structures, performativity, visuality, the contingency of subject/object positions, and a host of misrecognitions. But if this chapter attempted to theorize how plays are able to generate a more-or-less coherent subjectivity, Chapter 2 will investigate what one of these misrecognitions—the critical subject—might look like, however ambiguous it may turn out to be.

Notes

1. The 1958 film version of *Cat on a Hot Tin Roof* with Elizabeth Taylor and Paul Newman uses a console radio, which also broadcasts the play-by-play of a baseball game.

2. See Davy, "Constructing the Spectator," and Case, "Toward a Butch-Femme Aesthetic."

Works Cited

Auslander, Philip. "Liveness: Performance and the Anxiety of Simulation." *Performance and Cultural Politics*. Ed. Elin Diamond. London: Routledge, 1996.

Bakhtin, M. M. *Art and Answerability: Early Philosophical Essays by M. M. Bakhtin*. Ed. Michael Holquist and Vadim Liapunov. Trans. Vadim Liapunov. Austin: U of Texas P, 1990.

Barnes, Hazel E. "Translator's Introduction." *Being and Nothingness: A Phenomenological Essay on Ontology*. By Jean-Paul Sartre. New York: Washington Square, 1956.

Blake, Warner. *Voice of the Machine*. Newmark's Second Floor Gallery. June 13, 1996.

Butler, Judith. "Performative Acts and Gender Consitution: An Essay in Phenomenology and Feminist Theory." *Performing Feminisms: Feminist Critical Theory and Theatre*. Ed. Sue-Ellen Case. Baltimore: Johns Hopkins UP, 1990.

Case, Sue-Ellen. "Toward a Butch-Femme Aesthetic." *Making a Spectacle: Feminist Essays on Contemporary Women's Theatre*. Ed. Lynda Hart. Ann Arbor: U of Michigan P, 1989.

Chambers, Jane. *The Quintessential Image. Amazon Allstars: Thirteen Lesbian Plays.* Ed. Rosemary Keefe Curb. New York: Applause, 1996.

Davy, Kate. "Constructing the Spectator: Reception, Context, and Address in Lesbian Performance." *Performing Arts Journal* 10 (1986): 43-52.

Dean, Nancy. "Introducing *The Quintessential Image* by Jane Chambers." *Amazon Allstars: Thirteen Lesbian Plays.* Ed. Rosemary Keefe Curb. New York: Applause, 1996.

Elliott, Anthony. *Social Theory and Psychoanalysis in Transition: Self and Society from Freud to Kristeva.* Oxford: Blackwell, 1992.

Frayn, Michael. *Noises Off.* London: Methuen, 1982.

Freud, Sigmund. "Leonardo da Vinci and a Memory of His Childhood." *The Freud Reader.* Ed. Peter Gay. New York: Norton, 1989. 443-81.

Holquist, Michael. "Introduction: The Architectonics of Answerability." *Art and Answerability: Early Philosophical Essays by M. M. Bakhtin.* Ed. Michael Holquist and Vadim Liapunov. Trans. Vadim Liapunov. Austin: U of Texas P, 1990.

Honneth, Axel. "Integrity and Disrespect: Principles of a Conception of Morality Based on the Theory of Recognition." *Political Theory* 20.2 (1992): 187-201.

Huyssen, Andreas. *After the Great Divide: Modernism, Mass Culture, Postmodernism.* Bloomington: Indiana UP, 1986.

Jay, Martin. *Downcast Eyes: The Denigration of Vision in Twentieth-Century French Thought.* Berkeley: U of California P, 1993.

Kristeva, Julia. *The Kristeva Reader.* Ed. Toril Moi. New York: Columbia UP, 1986.

Lacan, Jacques. *The Four Fundamental Concepts of Psychoanalysis.* Trans. Alan Sheridan. Ed. Jacques Alain-Miller. New York: Norton, 1978.

Laclau, Ernesto, and Chantal Mouffe. *Hegemony and Socialist Strategy: Towards a Radical Democratic Politics.* London: Verso, 1985.

LeCompte, Elizabeth. "Interview with Elizabeth LeCompte." "An Examination of Closed-Circuit Television Integrated into Avant-Garde Theatre Performance." John W. Newhouse. Ph.D. dissertation, New York U, 1988. 227-46.

McLuhan, Marshall. *Essential McLuhan.* Ed. Eric McLuhan and Frank Zingrone. New York: Basic Books, 1995.

Nealon, Jeffrey T. *Alterity Politics: Ethics and Performative Subjectivity.* Durham: Duke UP, 1998.

Sartre, Jean-Paul. *Being and Nothingness: A Phenomenological Essay on Ontology.* Trans. Hazel E. Barnes. New York: Washington Square, 1956.

States, Bert O. "The Phenomenological Attitude." *Critical Theory and Performance.* Ed. Janelle G. Reinelt and Joseph R. Roach. Ann Arbor: U of Michigan P, 1992. 369-79.

Williams, Tennessee. *Cat on a Hot Tin Roof.* New York: Signet, 1985.

——. *Cat on a Hot Tin Roof.* Dir. Bill Kincaid. Southern Illinois University Carbondale. 1 Oct. 1999.

2

THE MEDIATIZED IMAGINARY
AND THE CRITICAL SUBJECT POSITION

The observation that postmodern drama is able to take a critical stance toward television and the media culture is unquestionable. This is, of course, the most prevailing subject position drama has negotiated with respect to the media culture throughout the later twentieth century, and is easily recognizable in the critical attitude expressed toward television by plays such as *An American Daughter* by Wendy Wasserstein. The project of this chapter is to examine some aspects of how this critical subject position is realized by focusing on the way plays can offer a contestation of the media culture, in particular the media's construction of images of the subject and the mediatized Imaginary order. The drama under discussion here critiques television by deconstructing the media image, challenging the commodification of human subjects, and contesting the ideology of the media or at least how ideology and its contingent nature is performed through the media. I have chosen to highlight plays written by members of marginalized groups who have been cast traditionally as other in Western culture. Because of the subject positioning these playwrights—Frank Chin, Philip Kan Gotanda, Luis Valdez, and Suzanne Maynard—have experienced, the critique offered by their plays is particularly pointed, and renders the issue of the subjectivity of drama and theater in this context very recognizable. These playwrights demonstrate that drama is able to negotiate an identity from which a critical discussion of the media's construction of images may proceed. However, they also show how mediatized images such as the Lone Ranger, Frank Sinatra, and Mary Richards (Mary Tyler Moore) are not and cannot be coherent images of identity for any human subject. This sort of drama provides a critical, indeed even an angry, agency in a world seemingly swept ever further into mediatization.

However, my project is also not quite that straightforward. Such plays also demonstrate that postmodern drama finds itself in a complex, highly ambivalent position with respect to television and the media culture, and illustrate that drama and its performance in the theater is very much a Kristevan subject-in-progress, its identity a matter of constant renegotiation. While it may contest, parody, satirize, or attack the media's construction of images, drama also constructs and always has constructed images and contributed to an Imaginary order through its own mirroring apparatus as discussed in Chapter 1. In fact, some of the most deconstructive of contemporary plays attempt to undo stereotypical images of the other that the stage was initially responsible for producing. David Henry Wang's 1988 play, *M. Butterfly,* is a prime example. The stereotypical image of the Asian other that Wang takes apart first appeared in David Belasco's 1900 play *Madam Butterfly* and ultimately was popularized in the musical theater—the opera by Puccini. In another celebrated example, the Wooster Group's 1981 play, *Route 1 & 9 (The Last Act)*, attempted to use blackface to deconstruct Thornton Wilder's ideal image of small town, white America in *Our Town*; but the deconstruction backfired, being misread by audience members as resurrecting the racist images of African Americans that theater had previously constructed in its minstrel shows of the nineteenth century. As an unfortunate result, the Wooster Group's funding for the play was pulled (Savran 10).

The Wooster Group's experience with *Route 1 & 9* illustrates not only the fact of drama's ability to construct images, but also how easy it is to cross the border, even inadvertently, from what may be intended as a critical deconstruction back into a construction. For any playwright or director working today in the context of such images, whether theatrical or televisual, the terrain of identity politics is truly treacherous. Because of the contingent nature of the Imaginary and our inability to control the reverberation of meaning in dramatic signs or images, the position we negotiate today may very well be what we criticize tomorrow, and in the case of *Route 1 & 9,* tomorrow came all too quickly.

This highly charged situation is due in large part to the functions of representation itself. As shown in the previous discussion of Michael Frayn's *Noises Off,* representation always remains intact whether one is examining the "backside" or the "frontside" of theater. There is no position on the outside of representation from which to launch a critique, no site of "before," no site of "after" unless representation is to collapse completely, in which case there simply is no performance at all. Metadrama, for instance, comments on the dramatic, semiotic, and representational qualities of a play, but always from the position of being inside the play. What drama can do is work within the parameters of representation, invoke *différance* in its semiotic systems, allow a variety of meanings, some contradictory or oxymoronic, to reverberate through its images, contest ideologies and expose their contingent character, practice an undoing without undoing itself, and hope that all of this is readable to an audience.

Nevertheless, these functions contribute to an endemic irony in drama toward its own limits of representation and construction of images and in part underpin the ambivalent shifting in position plays take toward other representational systems such as television and the media in general. In some drama, this ambivalence takes the form of a playful, transformational, even celebratory approach toward television, particularly if the plays admit to the contingent, relational quality of ideological subject positioning. Most of the time, drama is indeed negotiating more than one subject position—although one may be dominant—and these subject positions may be critical and celebratory at the same time. For example, the play I discuss at the end of this chapter—*The Handwriting, the Soup and the Hats*—while contesting the mediatized Imaginary also suggests that the mediatized Imaginary may not be so bad after all.

I use the term mediatized Imaginary to describe the order in which the media culture constructs its collective images of selfhood and mirrors them back to the subjects of a community. That such an order has a profound impact on the negotiation of human subjectivity goes without saying. John L. Caughey argues in *Imaginary Social Worlds: A Cultural Approach* that today our culture defines the public's relationship to media figures such as baseball players, movie actors, and television news anchors as primarily social (40). Not only are we required to have a working knowledge of a vast array of media personalities just to engage in water-cooler conversations, but we also treat media figures as others who, through a social relationship, help define personal identity. This phenomenon goes some way toward explaining the worldwide outpouring of grief at the death of Princess Diana in 1997, a media figure who had developed a social rapport with millions of strangers and who mirrored their problems, hopes, and fears. Caughey points out that people will carry this subjectifying process to its extreme conclusion by restructuring their own identities as the identity of the media figure (57-58). Elvis impersonators are an obvious example. In terming this type of relationship an "imaginary social world," Caughey is pointing to a feature of postmodern life that goes by a number of names—imperial Imaginary, national Imaginary, social Imaginary, cultural Imaginary—names that I am collecting under the one umbrella of "mediatized Imaginary."

In fact, the range of imaginaries covered by the mediatized Imaginary is recognizable across a number of critics whose work focuses on the media. John Caughie, for instance, uses two of these terms—"cultural imaginary" (44) and "international imaginary" (46) in "Playing at Being American: Games and Tactics." In this essay, Caughie describes an Imaginary order that has to do with the construction of individual subjectivity in relation to a broad community of others, specifically the way images of the United States and Great Britain as national identities are sent round the world by the media. The relationship (non-American) others develop with this imaginary portrait he defines as one of "playing at being American" (44). Ella Shohat and Robert Stam use the term "imperial imaginary" to describe a similar cultural phenomenon—the media spectator in a global situation—and, like Caughie, go on to insist that such an order is available to resistance and open to negotiations of identity (Shohat and Stam 166-67; Caughie 55). Debbora Battaglia's "cultural imaginary" describes the construction of an American, Franklinian subject by the media during a recent debate over the issue of cloning. As she points out, in critiquing the potential objectification and commodification of the subject raised by the issue of cloning, the media has argued for the value of an autonomous, essentialized, naturalized, "self-made" self, a view of individual identity deeply embedded in the cultural Imaginary of Americans.

But, as Gail Valaskakis argues, this sort of Imaginary—what she terms a "social imaginary"—cannot possibly manage a diverse range of identities. In recounting the 1990 Mohawk warrior barricade in Quebec, Canada, she discusses how the media created a fictive warrior figure, how numbers of Native youth invested subjectivity in this single, dominant identity, and how it ultimately failed as an accurate reflection of the community (70-71). And Stuart Hall in "Cultural Identity and Cinematic Representation" coins the terms "European imaginary" and "Caribbean imaginary" to describe the figure of Africa in the European and Caribbean mind respectively (72, 76). More overtly than the other critics I have described above, Hall connects these images and their function in the subjectifying processes of cultural identity to the Imaginary in Lacanian theory (80). However, all of the above-cited Imaginary realms may be seen as extrapolations of Lacan's Imaginary order to a larger collective that has to do with communal identity, the media and how individuals "find themselves" in it. The Imaginary at this societal or cultural level becomes a reservoir of constructed images that attempt to mirror more or less coherently the selfhood of the subjects of a given community. And certainly, whether the self mirrored is essentialized (or not), and whether the process of mirroring is essentializing (or not) is a concern that constantly haunts the work of the above critics.

Indeed, Stuart Hall in his essay locates both an essentialized view of cultural identity as a collective "one true self" and a non-essentialized view that recognizes differences, histories, and subject positionings (69, 70-72). Interestingly, the above critics in their own ways present both of these perspectives on subjectivity. Perhaps it is most clearly recognizable in the work of Battaglia and Valaskakis, where, in showing how the media construct a collective selfhood that is essentialized as "one true self"—Franklin's self-made man or the First Peoples warrior— they also show how that subjectivity does not correspond to a relational or diverse community of identities. This lack of "fit" between the images presented by the media and the receiving subjects precisely creates the sort of negotiable space Caughie and Shohat and Stam recognize as a playful or transformational site of cultural identity. These critics would agree that the mediatized Imaginary, like the Lacanian Imaginary, even when playing an essentializing role or attempting to generate an essentialized self, is fraught with all sorts of fissures and gaps.

The fact that the above discussions recognize cracks in the character of the mediatized Imaginary illustrates the influence of such post-Lacanian social theorists as Louis Althusser and Ernesto Laclau and Chantal Mouffe. In brief, Althusser reads the traditional Marxist notion of ideology as a reflection of the forces of production through a Lacanian-type Imaginary order. In his view, ideology provides a mostly coherent mirror image for the subjects of capitalist society which covers over their "real" conditions of existence. Ideology operates, like Lacan's Imaginary, as misrecognition.[1] Advancing Althusser's theory somewhat further, Laclau and Mouffe recognize the contingent, highly variable and relational nature of hegemonic discourse, the lack of grounding for the social, and the existence of fissures in sociosymbolic reality.[2] While I do not want to argue that the mediatized Imaginary is simply ideology deployed through the landscape of the media culture, for I hope to retain the expressly Lacanian sense of this order, it is nevertheless clear that the mediatized Imaginary and the post-Lacanian concept of ideology overlap as realms of constructed images and misrecognitions of subjectivity in a community. To the fragmentary subject, the mediatized Imaginary, like ideology, is a funhouse of mirrors, a contingent order not wholly controllable and certainly open to challenge and to change.

But how do the media go about operating in an Imaginary order in the first place? This explanation begins in classic film theory of the 1970s and 1980s, in which Christian Metz and others argue that film works on the basic principle of generating a Lacanian-type mirror image for the viewer-subject. Acknowledging the supremacy Western culture reserves for the visual, film theorists describe how the spectator first identifies with the act of looking embodied in the camera and then with the object under observation. Through a series of camera shots and reverse shots, which provide a way of seeing through the eyes of some character, the spectator is "sutured" into an identification—

always a misrecognition—with the protagonist. As Sandy Flitterman-Lewis points out, the spectator is drawn into an imaginary world that has already been created for him or her (215), a situation very similar to the way the mediatized Imaginary is already in place for the subject. This filmic Imaginary order is fundamentally how critics understand the way film generates its viewer-subject.

Later theories have been derived from film criticism to explain the basic subjectifying operations of theater and television. Theater also depends on the audience's training in a visual culture to create an identification with the act of looking, although of course this process is not governed by a camera's series of shots. Nevertheless, by watching (and hearing) the imaginary world created on stage, the viewer is drawn into identifications with the characters of a play because they reflect back images of the viewer's subjectivity. The viewer literally undergoes a construction of his/her own identity through the performance of the actors. Perhaps more so in theater than in film, there is, however, a great deal of vulnerability associated with this enterprise, and consequently a number of avenues available for playfulness. The Brechtian alienation effect, for instance, in which the audience is deliberately made to feel estranged from the characters, is generated to a large extent by denying the audience's desire to undergo a theatrical mirror phase.

Television theorists also argue that it is primarily the viewer's act of looking, and to a lesser extent listening, that generates entry into an Imaginary order. But because of the interruptive quality of television programming with its constant insertion of advertisements, television has to rely less on the camera's sustained shot/reverse shot series and more on the circulation and repetition of video images for its subjectifying effects. By watching the same images—the sitcom characters, the news anchors—reflecting back over and over, the viewer is sutured first into a recognition of the television "people" and then into identification with them. Caughey's imaginary social world begins to develop as television draws the viewer ever further into the fantasy landscape where the televisually constructed images perform their function of mirroring a viewer selfhood, however problematic that selfhood may be. While we can say that identity is built in this realm, we must also admit that identity always turns out to be inadequate, in part simply due to failures inherent in the Lacanian Imaginary itself and in part due to television's tendency to reduce complex characters to type.

A good example of the way in which the media and television in particular go about constructing a mediatized Imaginary is the Ken Burns documentary on the Lewis and Clark expedition, first broadcast on PBS in the fall of 1997. Very like the media's construction of a Franklinian self-made man in the cloning debate, Burns produces a Jeffersonian selfhood, a scientific, democratic, adventurous, manly spirit that not only governs the ethos of the expedition, but is also reflected in the characters of Lewis and Clark. Lewis and Clark are quite literally made to perform Jeffersonian man out on the American frontier, and there are all sorts of comparisons to the Apollo moon expeditions to make this performance current. Indeed, the fact that Burns, his narrator, and his historians are interested in constructing a current Imaginary of the American self through the offices of television is made clear in the events they choose to particularize and their subsequent commentary.

For instance, they describe at length the decision-making process the corps used to determine their second wintering ground in which everyone, including Sacajawea, the Native American woman, and York, Clark's slave, was given the right to vote. The narrative treats this event as the reflection of an ideal America, "a quintessential American moment," and specifically attributes its democratic nature to the truly American character of Lewis and Clark: "It was Lewis and Clark at their best, which is America at its best." Such events in the documentary work toward building an Imaginary order in which images of a country, a nationhood, and a national identity are reflected back to the viewer and offered up for recognition and suturing, and are delivered, moreover, at a time when Americans feel profoundly uneasy about what constitutes American identity. In other words, the television show produces a fairly coherent Imaginary that nevertheless does not quite cover over the complex, fragmentary condition of American identity today, or even of Jefferson's own time, and performs what I think is safe to call an ideological misrecognition. And this particular mediatized

Imaginary of the American national self is just one among a whole gamut of mirrored selves—working, family, feminine, masculine—that television is continually constructing and putting forth.

Moreover, there are real problematics associated with these televisual images of the self. Because the style of television tends to typify, even stereotypify, the characters on its shows are not particularly multi-dimensional; on the other hand, because television usually employs realistic, often location sets, real people, and a realistic style of dialogue and acting, these typified characters are also endowed with the appearance of reality. The characters that emerge from these conflicting tendencies are simultaneously highly seductive and dangerously inadequate in terms of suturing and identification, for the viewer ends up circulating desire through a necessarily reductive image of selfhood. This is a point of criticism of television and the media out of which drama has generated a striking subject position, and is well illustrated by Frank Chin's play *The Chickencoop Chinaman*, first performed in 1972 at the American Place Theatre in New York City.

This play attacks the mediatized Imaginary by offering up for ferocious examination a number of media images of selfhood. Because the characters are Asian-American, it is easy to see how the media images of selfhood available to them really do not correspond well at all to their subjectivity, and thus how problematical the mediatized Imaginary really is. The most intriguing and unsettling of these media figures is the Lone Ranger, presented in the play as the early radio character but known to most of us as the "masked man" of 1950s television. For those of us who grew up watching or listening to the show, the Lone Ranger offered a fairly reductive image of the national self—heroic, civilizing, and manly—an earlier version of Burns's Jeffersonian man. But, as the play shows, it was made more difficult for someone like Tam, the main character and an aspiring filmmaker, because in a radio sea of white "All-American" boys, he could not find an Asian-American hero. He ended up settling on the Lone Ranger as an image of selfhood, because he could imagine that the Lone Ranger hid Asian eyes under his mask, and thus he could misrecognize himself in the Lone

Ranger's face. The Lone Ranger performed the function of mirroring back to Tam an Asian-American subjectivity, in which the Western element was figured as a mask or persona covering over an Asian essentialism.

But when the Lone Ranger shows up in act 2 of the play, Tam says, "did I ever tellya, I ever tellya the Lone Ranger ain't a Chinaman?" (31). The Lone Ranger turns out to be not only white, but a racist and drug addict to boot, which deconstructs the heroic national character for all members of the audience. But, doubly significant to Tam, the Lone Ranger is also shown as unable to reflect Asian-American essentialism, because the fundamental Asian element is shown to be absent under the mask, leaving Tam without a core of identity, peering into a subjectivity defined as a void. Indeed, the Asian-American subject in this play, or "Chinaman" as Tam calls it, is nothing more than a concoction of junk culture, assembled out of "railroad scrap iron, dirty jokes, broken bottles" and the language of "everybody else's trash" (6-7).

This is definitely the point Tam tries to make to the Hong Kong Dream Girl, another important media image in the play. Tam draws this seductive figure out of his imagination, where she offers a mediatized Imaginary of Asian-American womanhood, a sexy, Westernized femininity dressed in majorette costume and based on "a popular American song of the twenties" (3). Even though Tam is attracted to this "doll-like, and mechanical" figure (5), she too represents a misrecognition of Asian essentialism promoted by the mediatized Imaginary, an Asian rootedness overwritten by Western semiotics. The play aptly exposes how these media images of the Hong Kong Dream Girl and the Lone Ranger are indeed desirable, but because of their reductive, essentialist, and even racist nature can never correspond to Tam's contingent subjectivity—fragmentary, all language, and all performance.

The Chickencoop Chinaman positions itself as "angry play," and Tam as angry character. Curiously, his ability to understand the "real" nature of his own subjectivity does not abate the vexed feelings he harbors toward the mediatized Imaginary, both desiring and hating it right through to the ending of the play. And like the play, Tam remains trapped in the identity of the chickencoop chinaman, an identity which ultimately has been constructed and negotiated by the theatrical discourse. *Yankee Dawg You Die,* written a number of years later by Philip Kan Gotanda, is also "angry play," but offers a more complex critique of the mediatized Imaginary. Premiering in 1988 at the Berkeley Repertory Theater, the play shows how we desire media images, feel put off by their constitution, want to attain them anyway, and feel angry when they remain beyond our reach. This play emphasizes what *The Chickencoop Chinaman* hinted at regarding the performative aspect of our relation to the media culture: the mediatized Imaginary is something performed for us and performed by us, whether on television, in the theater, or in "reality."

Since the two characters of *Yankee Dawg,* Vincent Chang and Bradley Yamashita, are actors, the performative element is always shown to lie at the core of their struggle with the mediatized Imaginary. This fundamental condition is immediately made clear in the opening scene, "Interlude I," in which Vincent is revealed "portraying a 'Jap soldier'" in a 1940s-era movie. The "slanty eyes" of Sergeant Moto and his cartoonish accent, which does not correspond to the fact he graduated from the University of California, Los Angeles, offer one version of the stereotypical media image of the Asian male, in this case a post–World War II mediatized Imaginary, a number of which are presented or referred to in the course of the play: Charlie Chop Suey, whom Bradley calls "a Chinese Steppin Fetchit," for instance (6, 20-21).

Vincent and especially Bradley, the younger of the two men, feel most angry at the constitution of these sorts of media images of the Asian male, which are white reflections of Asian identity and whose purpose is, in actuality, to bolster white identity based on racial difference and national boundary. Naturally, they are far from accurately mirroring the subjectivity of Asian Americans, and indeed the ideological misrepresentation involved in such media images is evidenced in the plea Vincent makes as the "Jap soldier"—"Why can't you see me as I really am?" (6).

Unfortunately, performing a stereotypical media image of the Asian male is one of the few doors that is open to Vincent and Bradley if they want work as actors, and this situation forms the basis of their conflict as well as forming a major critical subject position for the play. Vincent wants to work even if it means he has to perform outrageous, Sergeant Moto–type characters; Bradley, on the other hand, wants to fight these stereotypical images, refusing at least at the beginning of the play to agree to roles that perpetuate them. As with Tam in *The Chickencoop Chinaman,* there is a complicated circuitry of desire and hate for the mediatized Imaginary going on in these characters, and a tremendous guilt that they, through their performances, construct stereotypes which are played out in the daily life of Asian Americans, including their own. In this way, the play demonstrates that the media image is very much a product of performance, and that the cultural and individual subject is not only performed by the mediatized Imaginary but that the mediatized Imaginary is also performed by the subject.

Indeed, the sort of stereotypical Asian character Vincent has performed has played a major role in forming the mediatized Imaginary for Bradley, because Bradley has been watching Vincent on television since his childhood. In these roles, Vincent formed a hero for Bradley, mainly because his was one of the few Asian faces on television. In fact, Bradley describes how he was so desperate in his youth for an Asian-American, media hero-figure that he misrecognized the name of the pop singer Neil Sedaka as Japanese-American (20) in much the same way Tam in *The Chickencoop Chinaman* misrecognizes the Lone Ranger. But Vincent must have made a confusing image of selfhood, because the television shows Bradley saw him in were old films or old episodes of *Bonanza.* Vincent would have been playing the sort of Sergeant Moto role that Bradley objects to so vehemently. Indeed, wasn't Vincent playing the subservient Chinese cook, Hop Sing, on *Bonanza,* the sort of character Bradley later describes as an emasculated house boy? The inadequacy of these media images is driven home in Bradley's fascination with one other childhood Asian hero-figure—Godzilla—a reductive image of the subject if ever there was one. Nevertheless, Bradley describes how he "crav[ed] for a hero, for a symbol, for a secret agent" (33), and found it in *Godzilla* on *Creature Features,* a media image who would be powerful and "manly" enough to take revenge for Bradley on racist whites, who would be exactly the opposite of Vincent's emasculated characters. Interestingly, the little white girl Bradley pictures Godzilla stomping on for calling him a "dirty Jap" learned the racist epithet from the same sort of old war movie Bradley has been watching on TV and in which Vincent has been working (34).

However, in a fascinating twist there turns out to be another mediatized Imaginary operating in *Yankee Dawg,* not just the media image of the stereotypical Asian male. At the end of the conversation discussed above, in which Bradley reveals how he worshipped Vincent as his television hero, Vincent confesses that his hero was Fred Astaire (15). Invariably, the mediatized Imaginary that Vincent, and Bradley as well, look to as positive consists of white male images, although Bradley would surely protest this at least at the beginning of the play. For instance, when Vincent wants to compliment a Chinese-American singer he compares him to Frank Sinatra (26). And Vincent has apparently "worn" the noses of a cavalcade of white, male stars: "Sinatra, Montgomery Clift, Troy Donahue—whatever was *in* at the time" (11), as Bradley accuses. Recognizing that such fashionable facial features, clearly a stereotype of the white male, form the Western benchmark of masculine beauty at any given time enables the play to bring up the issue of facial reconstruction, or as Bradley puts it, "Cutting up your face to look more white" (25). And, again, the issue of facial reconstruction is rendered more intensely by the fact that Vincent and Bradley are working in the media culture; they want to act, and if the white, male face is privileged, they know their careers ought to advance if they imitate the face.

Moreover, the issue of facial reconstruction ably exposes the circulation of desire going on between the human subject and the mediatized Imaginary. Nowadays, if identification with the mediatized Imaginary does not occur particularly well, if the image in the mirror of the media does not reflect back a very coherent picture of one's subjectivity, one can always change one's face. The most obvious person who has played out this scenario is the pop singer Michael Jackson, a black media star who has undergone many surgeries to restructure his face, and arguably his cultural and racial identity, as white. But such scenarios have also been played out by all kinds of white people;

even a television star like Roseanne Barr has reconstructed her face to create a more aesthetically pleasing version of the stereotypical white female face, in her case some combination of the features of Debbie Reynolds and Raquel Welch. Indeed, the examples of Michael Jackson and Roseanne Barr demonstrate Caughey's point in *Imaginary Social Worlds*: that the desire for a constructed image can loop back to engender the construction of the subject as that image.

It is interesting that, in these cases, the "suturing" of the surgically incised face seems to generate better suturing with the mediatized Imaginary. And if the subject is available to construction, performance, and identification with the mediatized Imaginary, the notion of an essentialist, natural, collective "one true self" seems to fly right out the window. If *The Chickencoop Chinaman* discovers a fragmentary "Chinaman" subject underneath the mask of Asian-American identity, *Yankee Dawg* uncovers an ineffable trauma, which seems akin to an encounter with the Lacanian "Real" or perhaps the Kristevan "True-Real," underneath the face presented to the public.

This encounter happens at a critical juncture in the play for Bradley, several scenes after he is denied a non-Asian role in a new television series and several scenes before he admits to Vincent that he, too, has now had his nose surgically redone. In "Interlude 6," Bradley describes a dream in which, during a death-like sleep, he offers bits of his own flesh to two vultures who circle over his "sleeping corpse" before they settle down to ripping him open (43). On the one hand, the dream probably represents the surgery Bradley underwent to reconstruct his face. He is quite literally offering up his flesh to be ripped open by the surgeons. At the same time, though, the dream also represents the trauma of subjectification taking place at the level of the body, a moment reminiscent of the threats of mutilation associated with the Oedipal rite of passage. In Bradley's dream, the body is not only being sacrificed to mutilation but has to undergo a form of death in order to reconstitute identity, to be "born again" to form a more perfect union with the media image. Bowing to this sort of change, to "cutting up [the] face to look more white," is so foreign to Bradley's conscious character that the event itself is cast as ineffable, and can only come "knocking," as Lacan would put it (56), in the form of a dream at the door of his unconscious mind. The trauma to the body is the same as the trauma to the subject and its subjectifying processes, and breaks through into Bradley's discourse only in what Kristeva calls a "hallucinatory icon" (230), the dream itself.

The issue of facial reconstruction, then, not only denies the essentialism of selfhood and collective "true" identity, but also points to something like the Real order the post-Lacanian Slavoj Žižek believes underlies all misrecognitions of the social, the traumatic kernel that comes "before subjectivation as identification, before ideological interpellation, before assuming a certain subject-position" (178). It also serves to critique Bradley for buying into the media culture and its demands, for becoming part of the deadness, the "sleeping corpse," of televisual discourse. Sure enough, at the ending of the play he is willing to perform the type of role Vincent has always played, the stereotypical Asian male in a new film entitled *Angry Yellow Planet*.

But *Yankee Dawg* also demonstrates that the mediatized Imaginary, because of its performative nature, is an exchangeable and, therefore, fluid and contingent phenomenon. If Bradley is finally playing Vincent's role, Vincent is finally playing Bradley's, looking for parts that depict the lives of ordinary Asian Americans, the sort of politically committed drama to which Bradley once aspired. This reversal between the two characters suggests that one mediatized Imaginary, a stereotypical Asian or white media image, can be exchanged for other constructions, and that drama is one of those transformational spaces described by Shohat and Stam in which such an exchange can be shown to take place. Indeed, *Yankee Dawg* offers itself as the prime example.

Curiously, though, the play also indicates that, even as theater must be seen as an arena like film and television in which images are constructed, television and film ought to be recognized as capable of offering a similar transformational space. The play does not simply negotiate a self-righteous "self" to the newer media. Near the ending of the play, Vincent describes the role he has taken in a Japanese-American film, in which he will play a character just like his father (49). He also describes, in what may have been an epiphany, a documentary on Martin Luther King he had recently watched on television. In this narrative, King comes to realize that he must fight "the slave inside of him," which Vincent recasts as "the 'ching-chong-chinaman'" (44). In other words, while contesting the media culture, the play also reveals a certain amount of ambivalence about it, suggesting that agency is available to the subject not only in drama but in television and film as well. Individual and collective identity are not simply predetermined by a passive ideology working through the Imaginary order of the media, but can be reconstructed and re-performed.

However, this sense of agency or of contingency in the media culture is not shown to be quite so available in Luis Valdez's play *I Don't Have to Show You No Stinking Badges!* Opening in 1986 by the Chicano theater group El Teatro Campesino and set during "the Reagan years, early in 1985" (156), the play is cast as a bizarre, nightmarish TV situation comedy about a Chicano family. Like Jane Chambers's *The Quintessential Image* discussed in Chapter 1, the stage is dressed as a TV studio with lights, microphones, and monitors, and the characters, most often Sonny, occasionally break off the action to converse with an offstage director. The audience plays the TV studio audience. To make the metadramatic layering of the play even more complex, the mother and father characters—Connie and Buddy Villa—are television and film bit actors who, like Vincent in *Yankee Dawg,* have managed to make quite a decent living out of playing stereotypical parts like the "wetback" gardener and maid. In fact, the title of the play comes from a line Buddy, as a Mexican bandito, speaks to Humphrey Bogart in the film *The Treasure of the Sierra Madre*—"I don't have to show you any stinkin' badges!" (158). (The line was actually spoken by Alfonso Bedoya.)

To be sure, the question of whether these characters have much mastery over the construction of their identities and much agency when it comes to their destinies is a matter of real concern to this play, and frankly, *Badges* seems to have complete confidence in the subject position it generates. The theater critics who initially reviewed the play apparently wanted it to offer more choice, at least to offer an alternative to life in the media culture, which is what the play most definitely represents. Despite acclaiming a number of brilliant moments in *Badges,* the reviewers more often detect flaws in the TV sitcom aspect and in the general project of the play, which they speak of, in a variety of terms, as muddled, murky, and baffling. Although they agree that the play is about "life on the hyphen," or life as Mexican-American, perhaps Sylvie Drake, reviewer for the *Los Angeles Times,* puts it best when she claims that "the central argument [in the play]—should we 'adjust' to life as stereotypes or should we fight it?—remains unresolved" (94: G1).

But, one could respond, why should the play resolve this argument? Indeed, why would we think it is even resolvable, especially taking into consideration the premise of *Badges*? Because of the television format of the play, its "reality" is a TV sitcom with the sitcom's tendency toward rendering character as reductive type; as Sonny reveals, it could be worse: "I'll keep this situation comedy from turning into a soap opera" (186). Moreover, because the play is about acting and actors in television and film, as in *Yankee Dawg* there may simply be no easy or realistic way for the characters to "fight" the sort of mediatized Imaginary they depend on for their livelihood. And, perhaps most importantly, the play really is about life as the media culture, or the media culture as life, or even life dreamt as the media culture. In fact, Judith Green of the *San Jose Mercury News* and Christine Arnold of the *Miami Herald* suggest that *Badges* is expressionistic, taking place "inside Sonny's head" (Green 94: G2) as a "dream world" (Arnold 78: F10). And there certainly is evidence for this interpretation when, for instance, Sonny is shown in dream-like sequences riding on a director's dolly or giving instructions to an invisible crew. Regardless, though, of whether we should understand the play as a character's vision or as the playwright's vision, the media culture portrayed in *Badges* does ultimately "script" what the characters do, no matter if they attempt to fight it or not. As the directorial voice tells Sonny at the ending of the play, "WHO SAID ANYTHING ABOUT REALITY? THIS IS TELEVISION. . . . IF IT CAN'T COME ACROSS IN BUFFALO, YOU CAN FORGET IT" (209-10).

What drives *Badges* is, of course, Sonny's attempt "to break through this ridiculous situation comedy" (200) and into some sort of meaningful "reality"; but as the logic of the play dictates, he can only break through into another "television show," a "Hill Street Blues" (203), complete with its own reductive images of the young Chicano. Instead of his achieving some sort of contact with a reality outside television, we find Sonny in act 2 not only playing out a fantasy scenario of holding up the local "Crap in the Box" as the stereotypical "East L.A. cholo" (198), but putting his life in the terms of televisual discourse: "Here's the main event: the indispensable illiterate cholo gang member-heroin-addict-born-to-lose-image, which I suppose could account for 99% of my future employment in TV land. Just look hostile, dumb, and potentially violent" (199).

In this example, the play not only renders a televisual "reality," but also exposes and criticizes the mediatized Imaginary of the Chicano to be found there. Throughout the play, identity is invariably put in the terms of media images; but what surprises is the type and variety of image the characters invoke. Whereas *Yankee Dawg* offers the reflective mirror of two basic media stereotypes—the Asian and white males—*Badges* runs a racial, national, and gendered gamut of collective, but typified selves. Constantly it happens in the play that the characters identify each other and themselves in reductive media and cultural terms. A particularly brilliant example occurs in act 1 which I will try to summarize below.

It begins with Buddy and Connie dressed for an audition as a Mexican gardener and maid. Buddy soon recasts himself in the fantasy role of Nigel Lopez, "sophisticated Chicano spy," product of an English/Mexican union (172). Over the next two or three minutes, the characters engage in a rapid-fire blitz of misrecognitions. Based on the name "Anita" of Sonny's Asian-American girlfriend, Buddy assumes she is a "French babe." A few lines later, Sonny accuses Connie of being "a Jewish mother," to which Connie retorts by calling him "Sergeant Preston of the Yukon." Suddenly noticing the outfits his parents are wearing, Sonny says, "What's this? 'The Grapes of Wrath'—in Spanish?" Buddy responds, "I'm just the wetback gardener. Who's Anita?" Connie answers, "A Chicana from New York? *Oy Vey*" (173-74). And then Buddy, expressing disapproval over Sonny's hair, says, "You look like a fugitive from a Cochise picture" (175). As this dialogue suggests, all of us are susceptible to the power and influence of media and cultural constructions of the other's collective identity. Indeed, some time later Connie bases her knowledge of the Japanese-American experience during World War II on such John Wayne movies as *Sands of Iwo Jima* and *Guadalcanal Diary* (191), an epistemology that Bradley of *Yankee Dawg* would surely despise.

It soon becomes clear that Sonny is the play's best example of a life being played out under the tyranny of the mediatized Imaginary, a character whose subjectivity is constructed imperfectly as a collage of media images. Not going as far as Vincent and Bradley in actually altering the facial features, Sonny nevertheless at one point provides a list of media figures—all white male—he identified with strongly enough in his youth to imitate in clothing style and behavior. He describes how he "wanted to be like John Travolta" after seeing *Saturday Night Fever,* going so far as to wear a white disco suit, and after seeing *Raiders of the Lost Ark* talking his parents into a trip to Mexico in search of Mayan gold. Tellingly, Sonny refers to himself as a "stumpy, brown Harrison Ford" (179). The most enduring figure on this list, though, is Charles Laughton in *Witness for the Prosecution,* which the Villas have seen on video "dozens of times" (179). It is this media image of the heroic lawyer that has sent Sonny to study pre-law at Harvard. But, perhaps not surprisingly, the Charles Laughton figure is more accurately representing the mediatized Imaginary of legitimatized, professional (white) success that Buddy and Connie envision for their son.

The fact that neither Charles Laughton nor the other media images can act as very coherent reflections of Sonny's subjectivity is brought home in his description of what it was like being a "Ha'va'd man," of having to fake a life in order to perform the mediatized Imaginary of "the GREAT AMERICAN SUCCESS STORY" (207). The great American success story at Harvard turns out to be Sonny's roommate, one Monroe James, whom Sonny sees as perfectly reflecting the subjectivity he desires: "Tall, rich, blond" (207). A white-Anglo-Saxon-Protestant, Monroe would seem to fit ideally the mediatized Imaginary of the successful American male to which Sonny is supposed to rise. But in a wonderfully cynical twist, the play demonstrates that not even

Monroe James, the true-blooded, WASP All-American, can achieve the sort of selfhood demanded by the collective Imaginary order. Sonny describes how he ran into their room late one night only to find Monroe blowing his brains out with a gun.

This horrible scene confirms to Sonny, and to the audience as well, that there is something going terribly wrong with the mediatized Imaginary. Like Tam in *The Chickencoop Chinaman,* Sonny describes how he uncovered a void beneath the image of selfhood he was trying so hard to construct. Interestingly, the terrifying epiphany occurs immediately prior to the suicide of Monroe and just when Sonny is struggling to write a perfect paragraph in English, the language that is supposed to open the door to achieving the version of success mirrored by the Charles Laughton character. First the syntax of his sentences breaks down and the spaces between the words become intolerable; he gets stuck on the hyphen between two words; then, when the hyphen disappears, he falls into a hole between the words, "into a sea of nothingness" (208). He discovers that language, or the Symbolic order, which is a fundamental aspect of creating the unconscious, indeed of creating the mediatized Imaginary itself, rides over a vast emptiness. And verifying just how empty that collective picture of selfhood really is becomes the purpose of the last act of Monroe James.

But in this crisis of language, *Badges* also seems to suggest that to lose the hyphen between two words may mean giving up "life on the hyphen," forgetting one's ancestry in favor of "this cheap imitation of Anglo life" (199). One interpretation of the play would understand Sonny's departure from Harvard and return to his L.A. neighborhood as an essentialist argument for the necessity of discovering one's true place in the collective "one true self" of Mexican-Americanness. And this reading is perhaps what the reviewers of the play were expecting to be able to give. Yet, like the other plays discussed so far, *Badges* does not let its characters or its audience off so easily. Sonny does return home, but only because he wants to work in Hollywood, to become an actor like and, of course, not like his parents, to play what he knows will be the stereotypical role of the "East L.A. cholo," to star in the TV sitcom that is the play itself. He wants to become a director like Woody Allen (184), who in this context simply represents another media image of the American success story updated to the 1980s, but less WASPish than Charles Laughton. However, perhaps most revealing of Sonny's continuing desire to construct subjectivity out of media images and of the play's refusal to provide an essentialist definition of identity is his statement that he wants to become "the newest superstar in Hollywood" (184). In other words, while the play continually demonstrates the deconstruction of media images, instead of pointing toward an essentialist grounding, it constructs other media images in their place. We end up in a Chinese box of layers, a figure that not only stands for the problematic of representation and the impossibility of getting outside it, but also involves theater as an object of this critique. If everything has been put back into the performative realm, the performative realm turns out to be theater.

The mediatized Imaginary is, of course, constructed by the media and performed by actors and other media figures; at the same time, as *Badges* so ably points out, the mediatized Imaginary also performs the subject, represented here by the members of the Villa family—actors and theatrical constructs themselves. But, the question arises, if we are back in the performative realm, why does *Badges* seem so much more deterministic than *Yankee Dawg?* After all, if both plays are illustrating the performative nature of the media image and the construction of dramatic images, how can *Yankee Dawg* seem more ambivalent, offering agency to the subject and an escape from the media culture while *Badges* seems unable to offer either?

Actually, *Yankee Dawg* does not really offer an escape from the media culture. If Vincent and Bradley want to work in the media culture, they are of necessity within it. Moreover, if Vincent does perform in the politically committed theater he will do so with his reconstructed face. Rather, the play offers a way to maneuver inside the media culture by suggesting that the subject can construct other, more multi-dimensional selves than the usual stereotypical products of the media. But it is still quite obvious that *Badges* does not offer even this much agency. A far greater sense of technological determinism—a belief in the fatalistic scripting of individual and collective life by the media— goes on in this play than in *Yankee Dawg,* a position on the media that has been popular throughout the twentieth century. *Badges* is not necessarily more critical of television and the media culture than *Yankee Dawg,* but it is certainly more cynical about what the subject can do given the confines of a TV sitcom and the way character is commodified to meet the narrow demands of the marketplace. Moreover, theater does not construct the role of a transformational site in this play. Quite the contrary: the play demonstrates that theater, ironically, is ultimately responsible for creating the images in the play, even the stereotypical media images.

This cynicism is undoubtedly embedded in the play's ending, when the logical conclusion—Sonny's act of shooting himself—is cut by the director. To make a statement that a life governed by media images is intolerable would render the sitcom not light enough, not entertaining enough, not funny enough for television. The director replaces the scene with Sonny and Anita taking off in a giant sombrero–flying saucer while Buddy and Connie finish the play in a romantic 1940s movie kiss. And really, if one thinks about it, the suicide scene would have afforded no real alternative anyway, since such scenes of violence are also highly amenable to televisual discourse. The fundamental problem with having Sonny commit suicide is that a TV sitcom has to re-produce its main character week after week. And, to be sure, flying saucers always go over well on television. Seriously, though, in showing how Sonny not only complies with this ridiculous ending but indeed helps create it, the play continues to demonstrate right out to the curtain not only the politics of technological determinism, but also the way theatrical images are constructed and implicated.

On the other hand, *Badges* does not actually deny the notion of agency for the subject in general: Monroe James is certainly able to pull the trigger. It just does not show agency as being possible within the context of the media's or the play's imagistic entrapment. One of the main reasons for the difference in subject positioning of *Badges* and *Yankee Dawg* is that *Badges* has more of the hardness and incorrigibility associated with a certain type of postmodernism, the sort of icy, impenetrable exterior found in plays like David Mamet's *Glengarry Glen Ross.* One tends to skate around on the surface of such plays rather than delve into a deep structure, because the only thing made available that is remotely like a deep structure turns out to be a void. In *Yankee Dawg,* on the contrary, something lies at the bottom of the pit even if it is a trauma. In this respect, *Badges* is more similar to *The Chickencoop Chinaman* because everyone, from Sonny to Tam to the audience, is tossed back up to the surface after being provided with a glimpse of the emptiness riding underneath all the language, the games, the performances. *Badges* and *The Chickencoop Chinaman* derive this project from the sort of postmodernism initiated by absurdist drama, particularly Samuel Beckett's *Waiting for Godot,* in which Didi and Gogo perform their games on top of a surface that is covering "no lack of void" (42) while waiting endlessly for a Godot who perhaps does not even exist.

I would also suggest that the differences in subject positioning the plays express with respect to television and the media culture in general can be explained as political in the sense that attitudes taken toward the media are a product of negotiations and decisions made by the playwrights themselves. Throughout the twentieth century, from the moment film and then television were introduced to the present, there has been one extreme among culture watchers of taking a positive, more open approach to the newer media; there has been another extreme of viewing television and other electronic media as little more than vehicles for the worst banality of Western culture, the "vast wasteland" coined by Newton Minow, former chairman of the FCC. Even though *Badges, The Chickencoop Chinaman,* and *Yankee Dawg* are commenting on and critiquing the same cultural phenomena, they may be seen as occupying different sites along a political spectrum with *Badges* and *The Chickencoop Chinaman* residing closer to the negative end than *Yankee Dawg.* And while *Yankee Dawg* cannot be said to celebrate the media culture, the play does lean toward the positive pole more than the other two, because it concedes a certain degree of flexibility and changeability to the media, to drama, and to the mediatized Imaginary. To account for the different perspectives on television and the media in these plays may mean simply recognizing that the playwrights themselves have the agency to negotiate identity with respect to the media culture. Indeed, the final playwright I will discuss in this context exercises the most latitude in generating a dramatic "subject" that consists of critiquing but also appreciating television and the media culture.

Suzanne Maynard's *The Handwriting, the Soup and the Hats* is also a play about identity, particularly how the subjectivity of individuals fits into collective notions of subjectivity put forth by the media and, to a lesser extent, other related cultural phenomena. Presented in 1996 at Seattle's Annex Theatre, the play takes a critical but much less angry approach to television and the media culture than any of the other plays discussed in this chapter. Indeed, a veritable fondness can be detected even from simply perusing the production's program, which, like the play itself, is littered with playful references to television. The cover of the program features a drawing of a television set enclosing five repeating images of Marlo Thomas in her role as Ann Marie of the late sixties sitcom *That Girl,* and one frame of the opening sequence to the 1970s *Mary Tyler Moore Show* which shows Mary Tyler Moore as Mary Richards throwing her hat into the air. Inside the program are two additional photos of Marlo Thomas and Mary Tyler Moore in their respective characters as well as a campy reference to *Green Acres.* Moreover, the director, Andrea Allen, comments that the play reminds her of a happy childhood summer spent building a Barbie house and watching reruns of *That Girl* and *The Mary Tyler Moore Show* on television.

But is there any way to account for this play and its production's obviously more lighthearted, more celebratory approach toward television than the attitude expressed in the plays already discussed? It may have something to do with the fact that *Handwriting* is a more recent play, written and first performed in the mid-1990s. Television has now been around long enough to inspire a certain amount of nostalgia, to be treated as an old, albeit flawed, childhood friend. The play is also clearly a product of the contemporary period of cultural studies, when television is not only more likely to be taken seriously as a social phenomenon but is also seen as having cultural and aesthetic value. On the other hand, it is the case that *Badges* premiered not that much earlier than *Handwriting*—in the mid-1980s—when media studies was certainly well underway. Or, perhaps the friendlier treatment is due to the playwright's youth and inexperience: Maynard appears to be quite young and does not have many plays to her credit. On the other hand, Chin was only thirty-two when he wrote *The Chickencoop Chinaman,* his first play.

Handwriting is different—less angry at any rate—mainly because of the way it handles issues of race and gender. When the three characters of the play—all young, white women—look to Marlo Thomas and Mary Tyler Moore as representing a mediatized Imaginary of modern, single working woman, they see a fairly coherent image being reflected back. Not to the same extent are they faced with having to misrecognize deliberately a racial subjectivity underneath the mask of the Lone Ranger or in the name "Neil Sedaka." Notwithstanding the cases of Roseanne Barr and Monroe James, it is true that white people to a far greater extent than people of color are able to suture better with the white images of the Imaginary. Furthermore, the women of *Handwriting* do not have to deal with white images being presented in a racist fashion by the media. While Mary Richards may be a reductive and typified TV sitcom character, Sergeant Moto of *Yankee Dawg* is in a wholly different league.

Furthermore, *Handwriting* is less worried about issues of gender than either *The Chickencoop Chinaman* or *Yankee Dawg.* In Maynard's play, the empowerment of women represented by the liberating gesture of Mary Tyler Moore throwing her hat in the air is taken for granted. This play is a good example of what some critics call post-feminism. As Andrea Allen writes, "Years of Women's Studies courses later, I see the problems of Barbies and constricting female roles. But the Barbie I remember is not obscenely voluptuous. She is a doctor or a television producer or a director. She is going places." On the contrary, Chin and Gotanda's plays wrestle continually with the question of what it means to be "manly" in a Western culture that has feminized the Asian male. The fear of emasculation is always pressing.

In fact, race and gender become virtually inseparable issues in the two Asian-American plays. Tom in *The Chickencoop Chinaman* says, "In American eyes we don't appear as he-men types," to which Tam replies, "Oh, we look like queers!" (59). Similarly, in *Yankee Dawg* Bradley describes how he knifed a non-Asian man for making a derogatory sexual comment about his girlfriend, an insult he undoubtedly took as belittling his masculinity. Moreover, both plays target the media as largely responsible for the way notions of masculinity or its lack are purveyed to the public. The stereotypical white media images from the Lone Ranger to Frank Sinatra, for instance, are seen to represent "manly" men; but the Asian images always devolve into what Bradley calls "emasculated house boys." Indeed, Bradley rails at television in particular for the feminizing of the Asian male: "They fucking cut off our balls" (27). Television is certainly never accused of anything nearly so violent, mutilating, or Oedipal in *Handwriting,* in large part because Marlo Thomas and Mary Tyler Moore are much more positive images of the subject, in fact are better at the ideological project of filling in than any of the media figures offered in the other plays.

Nevertheless, television is definitely treated critically in Maynard's play, and shows how postmodern drama can become a site of important discussion of the media and the mediatized Imaginary. While all three characters—Annie, Gene, and Maura —struggle with questions of their identity, the mediatized Imaginary appears most clearly as a problematic mirror of subjectivity for Annie. Because Annie is an aspiring actress and spends a good deal of time in the play trying to perform the character of "Sara" (whom Gene, an aspiring playwright, is trying to write), she bears the focus as the subject who has identified most strongly with a performative, a media image.

From the opening lines of the play, Annie is referencing *That Girl* and Marlo Thomas as her childhood "hero" and role model: "I spent a good part of adolescence emulating *That Girl* and all that it foretold about adult life" (3). But the limitations of the mediatized Imaginary are brought out immediately when Annie defines a major difference between herself and the Marlo Thomas character: "she had canned laughter to back her up" (4). Indeed, when Annie describes how she lost her faith in Marlo Thomas by discovering that *That Girl* was a spinoff of *Love American Style,* she produces a deconstruction of the essentialism often seen in the mediatized Imaginary—the "one true self." The illusion of an originary selfhood, represented by Marlo

Thomas for, ironically, millions of girls, is demystified as a replicable image strung intertextually over at least three television shows, counting *The Mary Tyler Moore Show.* Indeed, the production's program is undoubtedly helping to make this point in the series of Marlo Thomas and Mary Tyler Moore images inside the TV set on the front cover.

Gene and Maura, who turn out to be long-lost sisters separated at the death of their mother, are also trying to construct identities, Gene out of a montage of faces cut from high school yearbooks, Maura out of a Cleaverized vision of the ideal American "television" family. As in *Yankee Dawg,* a traumatic experience turns out to underlie the fragmented subjectivity of the sisters: their mother died while giving birth to Maura, a fact that is of course nothing but a blank in Maura's memory and under erasure in Gene's, the older of the two. But what is really important about the play is the way the characters come to understand this event. Rather than seeing their mother's death as being *caused* by something—by fate, by an event, or by something someone did—they eventually realize that it was a product of randomness, as much due to "time and space and the pull of the tides" as anything else (19). Things happen out of what is available in the pool of things, rather than out of one cause giving rise to one effect.

And this notion of a pool of availability, a site of contingency, is the clearest alternative to identity politics any of these plays make. Human subjects devise a sense of self—a misrecognition—out of what is available to them, and the mediatized Imaginary is without a doubt available whether it comes in the form of Marlo Thomas, Mary Tyler Moore, or the cultural icon of Barbie. These images are shown to stand in for and mirror a fragmented subjectivity. They are not perfect, complete, or coherent; but in this play imperfection, incompleteness, and incoherence are considered "okay." For instance, even after demystifying the Marlo Thomas character, Annie continues to identify positively with *That Girl,* showing up in one scene in Ann Marie's pill-box hat (the significance of "the hats" in the play's title), and at the end of the play planning to marry her "Donald," her mediatized Imaginary boyfriend. Maura makes her final appearance happily Barbie-ized in her old prom dress.

Of the "subject(s)" that the four plays under discussion negotiate for drama and theater in general, *Handwriting* has the most ambivalent and contingent subjectivity. While it contests and critiques television, the play also celebrates television as an endearing character of the postmodern scene, and explores the position(s) for postmodern drama within this media matrix. The play acknowledges that its discourse and theatrical discourse in general are inside the representational parameters of the media as well as inside the frame of late-twentieth-century Western culture and literary movements. Indeed, all of the plays discussed in this chapter (as well as in the book) are historically contextualized, and display a generic agency within the parameters of culture and within a narrativized representation of drama history.

Importantly, all four plays acknowledge the imagistic nature of drama, and the way it makes, sustains, performs, and remakes Imaginaries, even those of the media culture it wants to deconstruct. And certainly, the four plays suggest individually and collectively that the negotiations drama conducts with television and the media culture for an identity do not produce an essentialist "one true self" for drama or production, or an originary subject, even though a limited range of subject positions—angry play, for instance—may dominate. Instead, to follow the lead of *Handwriting,* the media culture and its Imaginary(s) should be considered as a pool of availability, and postmodern drama should be reconsidered as a dynamic site of cultural transformation in which the subjectivity of genre and cultural institution is performed out of a series of acts rather than originated. Performative theory describes identity, to use an idea of Jeffrey Nealon, as a translation from the verb into the noun (126). The subject thus generated will always already be contingent, and agency always already subject to change.

Notes

1. See Louis Althusser's "Ideology and Ideological State Apparatuses" and "Freud and Lacan."

2. See Laclau and Mouffe's "Hegemony and Radical Democracy."

Works Cited

Althusser, Louis. "Ideology and Ideological State Apparatuses" and "Freud and Lacan." *Lenin and Philosophy and Other Essays.* Trans. Ben Brewster. New York: Monthly Review P, 1971.

Arnold, Christine. "'Badges' Is a Passionate Exploration of the Struggle to Join the Mainstream." *Miami Herald* 13 Oct. 1986: 78: F10.

Battaglia, Debbora. "Fear of Selfing in the American Cultural Imaginary or 'You Are Never Alone with a Clone.'" *American Anthropologist* 97.4 (1995): 672-78.

Beckett, Samuel. *Waiting for Godot.* New York: Grove, 1954.

Burns, Ken. *The Corps of Discovery: The Lewis and Clark Expedition.* PBS, 1997.

Caughey, John L. *Imaginary Social Worlds: A Cultural Approach.* Lincoln: U of Nebraska P, 1984.

Caughie, John. "Playing at Being American: Games and Tactics." *Logics of Television: Essays in Cultural Criticism.* Ed. Patricia Mellencamp. Bloomington: Indiana UP, 1990. 44-58.

Chin, Frank. *The Chickencoop Chinaman. The Chickencoop Chinaman and The Year of the Dragon: Two Plays by Frank Chin.* Seattle: U of Washington P, 1981. 1-66.

Drake, Sylvie. "'Badges' Punctuates the Hyphenated Life." *Los Angeles Times* 7 Feb. 1986: 94: G1.

Flitterman-Lewis, Sandy. "Psychoanalysis, Film, and Television." *Channels of Discourse, Reassembled: Television and Contemporary Criticism.* Ed. Robert C. Allen. Chapel Hill: U of North Carolina P, 1992. 203-46.

Gotanda, Philip Kan. *Yankee Dawg You Die.* New York: Dramatists Play Service, 1991.

Green, Judith. "Teatro Campesino's Comedy Verges on Melodrama." *San Jose Mercury News* 16 Feb. 1986: 94: G2.

Hall, Stuart. "Cultural Identity and Cinematic Representation." *Framework* 36 (1989): 68-81.

Kristeva, Julia. *The Kristeva Reader.* Ed. Toril Moi. New York: Columbia UP, 1986.

Lacan, Jacques. *The Four Fundamental Concepts of Psychoanalysis.* Trans. Alan Sheridan. Ed. Jacques-Alain Miller. New York: Norton, 1981.

Laclau, Ernesto, and Chantal Mouffe. "Hegemony and Radical Democracy." *Hegemony and Socialist Strategy: Towards a Radical Democratic Politics*. London: Verso, 1985.

Maynard, Suzanne. *The Handwriting, the Soup and the Hats*. Seattle: Rain City Projects, 1996. Annex Theatre, 14 July 1996.

Nealon, Jeffrey T. *Alterity Politics: Ethics and Performative Subjectivity*. Durham: Duke UP, 1998.

Savran, David. *The Wooster Group, 1975-1985: Breaking the Rules*. Ann Arbor: UMI Research P, 1986.

Shohat, Ella, and Robert Stam. "From the Imperial Family to the Transnational Imaginary: Media Spectatorship in the Age of Globalization." *Global/Local: Cultural Production and the Transnational Imaginary*. Ed. Rob Wilson and Wimal Dissanayake. Durham: Duke UP, 1996. 145-70.

Valaskakis, Gail. "Rights and Warriors: First Nations, Media and Identity." *ARIEL: A Review of International English Literature* 25.1 (1994): 60-72.

Valdez, Luis. *I Don't Have to Show You No Stinking Badges! Zoot Suit and Other Plays*. Houston: Arte Publico, 1992. 155-214.

Žižek, Slavoj. *The Sublime Object of Ideology*. London: Verso, 1989.

3

PERFORMING TELEVISION / THEORIZING PERFORMANCE

Postmodern drama has often interrogated television, as the previous chapter showed, from assessing its aesthetic value as a cultural form to critiquing its production of a mediatized Imaginary. But has television anything at all to say about drama and performance? Of course, television has often employed theatrical discourse and tropes—*American Playhouse, Masterpiece Theater,* for example—but is it possible for television to comment on the aesthetics of theater or to offer any sort of insight on its workings or its identity in the media culture? Taking network or cable television on their own, it is true that in these formats television regularly comments hyperconsciously on itself (witness the Simpsons plopping down on their couch to watch the credits of *The Simpsons* roll by), but rarely, if ever, comments on dramatic forms or other media such as film and radio.

Nevertheless, when television is incorporated into plays such as Megan Terry's *Home: or, Future Soap,* Lee Blessing's *Fortinbras,* or Don DeLillo's *The Day Room,* when theater literally "performs" television, a commentary about dramatic discourse is invoked by the televisual discourse. Intuitively, this assertion makes sense because, according to the theory developed in Chapter 1, all discussion by drama about television is ultimately a self-reflexive discussion and pertains, in particular, to the issue of the subjectivity and identity of postmodern drama and theater in a media culture. The project of this chapter is to examine, especially on the formal levels of semiotics, performativity, and spectatorship, what sort of commentary is generated by television and to map out the theoretical issues a televisual discourse opens up about drama and performance.

Theater and television as well as film have been subject to a great deal of theorizing over the last few decades. Since the three share certain features in common—they are visual, performative media, for instance—and since the theorists who discuss them tend to inhabit the same academic pool, as might be expected a number of the theories stem from the same theoretical foundations and in their applications overlap each other. Feminist, Marxist, and cultural critics from Laura Mulvey to Raymond Williams to Philip Auslander have produced numerous analyses of the gendering of television, drama and theater, and film and the tendency toward their commodification as cultural institutions. I have already demonstrated in Chapters 1 and 2 the way in which a post-structuralist theory of psychoanalysis can be used to discuss the dramatic arts and television in terms of identity and the Imaginary register, and certainly other critics such as Susan Bennett in *Theatre Audiences: A Theory of Production and Reception* and Barbara Freedman in *Staging the Gaze* adroitly use theories of spectatorship and the spectatorial gaze to conduct a conversation between theater and film.

Perhaps not surprisingly, most contemporary theoretical positions taken toward the media rest on structuralist or post-structuralist grounds. Humanist approaches have fallen away, with the noteworthy exceptions of Martin Esslin and Bert O. States's work. Semiotics as used by analysts such as Patrice Pavis and Keir Elam in drama and Ellen Seiter in television have contributed enormously to our understanding of the media as sign systems and the codes and messages at work in them. Furthermore, notions of performance or "the performative" as used by theorists such as Jeffrey Nealon introduce the visual media as texts that not only represent semiotically, but actually "do" something in the world. In a similar vein, narrative discourse has proven to be especially fruitful in unpacking the basic structure of the media. In television studies, for instance, the practice of using narrative analysis certainly goes back to 1974, when Raymond Williams first observed that broadcast television was based less on the notion of the discreteness of an item (a book, a play, or an event) than on the idea of a "flow" or a sequencing of such items (80-81). Flow has been one of the most influential ideas in television theory and has been updated by several later critics. In *The Social Semiotics of Mass Communication,* Klaus Bruhn Jensen develops the notion of three flows: a "channel flow" which is created by each station; a "super-flow" which combines all the channel flows; and a "viewer flow" which is created by what the viewer actually constructs out of the super-flow (109-10).

Flow has also been used to identify, as Williams himself does, one of the basic differences between television and all other cultural forms. Indeed, a common tactic employed by critics in developing theories about theater, television, and film is to describe the differences among some combination of the three performance genres. Most of these analyses center on the differences either between theater and film or between television and film; very few consider a comparison of theater and television. However, by extrapolating from several discussions, it is possible to arrive at the most relevant points of difference among the three media.

Visible Fictions by John Ellis is perhaps the best example of this comparative approach to theorizing about the media, and contains one of the most salient discussions of film and television to date. Following Williams, Ellis recognizes the discreteness of the single film text and the public nature of its performance (111). Of course, these features are also true of drama and theater: a play is most often experienced as a single text, and as Susan Bennett points out, also attended as a public event (80). Television, on the other hand, is watched in a domestic setting (Ellis 111), the privacy of the home. In contrast to the individualized nature of television viewing, film and theater share the feature of a group audience. However, only theater offers the possibility of direct communication between the actors and the audience, a shared "live presence" which allows the audience to interact with and modify the performance, as Bennett notes. She goes on to say that film, and we can add television, always has a camera interpreting the action and governing the audience, a situation that is quite different from theater's (80-81). And unlike film and television, which record their performances on film footage and videotape, theater is not perfectly and endlessly repeatable.

In terms of narrative structure, Ellis writes that film, especially the classic narrative genre, is constructed as consequential, according to "a chain of cause and effect," and features a central problematic that drives the narrative toward closure (76). Bert O. States makes essentially the same assessment of drama in *The*

Pleasure of the Play: most plays are based on the empirical sequencing of cause and effect with the "accident" offering the same sort of driving force as Ellis's problematic; together with the empirical design, an "entelichial" or formal logic leads to the "convergence" of the play's ending (65, 73), which again is similar to Ellis's filmic closure or "final coherence" (76). As States claims, even absurdist or deconstructive drama, which may appear to subvert probability, nevertheless has its own internal logic to follow (69-70).

On the other hand, Ellis argues, the structure of television is quite different. Rather than the single coherent text of film with its steady progression through events or, I would add, the narrative momentum developed over the several extended scenes of most drama, the building block of television is the segment. He defines the segment as brief "unities of images and sounds whose maximum duration seems to be about five minutes" (112). Certainly, a segment can be of much shorter duration—a twenty-second advertisement, for instance. Television assembles its narrative (both fictive and non-fictive) out of a rapid exchange of segments (120), a characteristic I have called a "play among texts." The uniqueness of this segmentalization to television, which Ellis characterizes as television's "distinctive aesthetic form" (112), with its rapidity of juxtaposition, cannot be underestimated, and is one of the main reasons why films and plays that are broadcast on television seem slow. The impression of slowness is due less to the viewer's short attention span than to his or her expectations of television's particular style and structure.

Ellis goes on to describe how the segment underlies the serial and series formats so basic to televisual narrative, with their continual repetition of character and situation (122-23), also a function of the repeatability in part promoted by the use of videotape. And rather than the problematic built into filmic narration with its eventual resolution, it is the open-ended dilemma and subsequent lack of closure that drives the television series onward. While Ellis is right in suggesting that the dilemma and its series format is probably the major contribution television has made to the history of narrative form (154), it is well to keep in mind that all narrative forms, because they are semiotic discourses, are subject to repetition and open-endedness. Even though absurdist plays like Beckett's *Waiting for Godot* may conclude or, as States would say, "converge," they are nevertheless based on repetition and the logic of the dilemma. As Patrice Pavis points out, avant-garde drama has used the serial format— the multiplication and repetition of the sign—as part of an effort to defeat the constraints of the sign (182-84).

Indeed, these differences in venue, audience, and narrative structure found among theater, television, and film are broad and general, and because they are categorical become somewhat fuzzier in practice. In other words, there is a certain amount of breakdown that occurs even among these fundamental differences and a lot of similarity to be found among the media as well. For instance, while it is true that the television series format has a continually deferred ending, each episode in that series invariably concludes with a strong sense of closure. The bad guys are caught and justice prevails each and every time (but, of course, over and over). In fact, one of the main reasons for the negative audience reaction to David Lynch's innovative 1980s series *Twin Peaks* was that each episode did not firmly close.

Or consider sports events. One would intuitively assume that seeing a game such as NHL hockey "live and in person" would be more exciting and dramatic than seeing it at home on television. But the contrary seems to be true. When I tried this experiment I found that at the arena the game was hard to see, difficult to follow, and devoid of anything more than the simplest Aristotelian dramatic form: beginning (first period); middle (second period); and ending (third period). Even the crowd, which was definitely more raucous than any theater audience I had ever heard, could not inspire the event. On television, though, the way the announcers cast the game, the marvelous camera angles with their close-ups and split screens, and the video slow motion replays infuse the game with drama. It becomes a contest between two warring sides almost Shakespearean in proportion, each with its talented but flawed leaders, their mistakes of hubris and heroic acts. And even though the televised event is constructed out of segments with numerous commercials and promos and is one game in a series of games, like a play or film it definitely drives toward an ending. It is ironic that television, in borrowing theatrical tricks of the trade, makes its mediated performance of hockey more theatrical than the "onstage" event.

Similarly, the public nature of theater and film with their defining feature of a group audience is not quite as delimited as the critics make it out to be. It is certainly possible to watch a movie home alone, and perhaps the biggest fear of any theater company is that only one person will show up for the performance. On the other hand, while it is true that television is usually watched alone or in very small groups, one can certainly go to a sports bar and see a game with a fairly large group audience. Indeed, at special times such as the World Series or Stanley Cup playoffs, thousands of fans go to the arena to watch on television the away games of their team, forming an audience that is often bigger than those attending Broadway musicals.

Nevertheless, the mediating action of the camera and recorded performance, the communal nature of the experience, and the audience and actors' shared "live presence," or lack of these elements, are undoubtedly major defining "grounds" of theater, television, and film. In fact, it is possible to see these differences at work when comparing theater and television versions of the "same" play, such as Samuel Beckett's *Krapp's Last Tape,* which was produced for television in 1990 as part of the *Beckett Directs Beckett* series. Of course, it is well documented how much Beckett was interested in television and other forms of media (Gussow 43). Indeed, *Quad* was written specifically for television, and several of his later plays such as *What Where* were re-figured by the playwright himself for televised performance.

When *Krapp's Last Tape* (*KLT*) was first broadcast in the United States on the Public Broadcasting Service (PBS), it was followed by a behind-the-scenes program on the making of the television production that included an interview with the actor who played Krapp, Rick Cluchey. It is clear from some of Cluchey's remarks that the television version attempts to preserve certain aspects of the theater performance. The play was recorded in one long, forty-two-minute take without cutaways or editing. Rather than relying on the televisual discourse of rapidly juxtaposed segments, the production maintained the extended scene of drama. On the other hand, the presence of a live audience—a factor so important to theatrical space—was removed. While the lack of a live audience reduces much of the tremendous vulnerability an actor feels on the stage, it also presented a real challenge to Cluchey. He describes the difficulty he experienced in having to act for the camera instead of to an audience, but in not being able to "go directly to the camera." Without the live audience, the actor in this situation plays to a void, which Cluchey interestingly terms "a wasteland." This choice of words is intriguing, for television has been saddled since the early 1960s with the moniker "a wasteland." However, in the context of Beckett's work, this particular play, and the style of the television production, the notion of a televisual "wasteland" may be a highly appropriate visual trope.

Here is why. The limits of Krapp's room and the circumscribed world he constructs in it form the wasteland of a life, which in turn may be interpreted in a variety of ways from a desolate physical or environmental landscape to a cultural, historical, artistic, or even temporal vacuum. (Katharine Worth points out that because the play is set in the future, Krapp has not actually reached the stage occupied by the image [18].) Moreover, when the play is performed in the theater, the stage serves as a physical sign of the wasteland by forming a spatial void in which Krapp and the play exist. In the television version, a very black screen effectively plays this role. In fact, at the beginning and ending of the television version, Krapp is located in the upper right corner of the screen, a placement that emphasizes the terrible loneliness of this minuscule figure who is drifting in a vast, black emptiness. Moreover, the physical shape of the stage and television set are used to enhance a sense of Krapp's entrapment. In both cases, Krapp is trapped in a box-like structure. However, perhaps the television version is more effective in lending a claustrophobic feel to this space, because of the use of close-up and medium camera shots. Often, just Krapp's face or his upper body and tape recorder fill the screen, making it look as if he has been squashed into the box. This metaphor of the wasteland as a total emptiness inside a small box is truly frightening, and cannot be created nearly as effectively in the theater version of the play. It depends too much on the camera's ability to alter the size of Krapp relative to the size of the playing area and to provide the spectator with more than one perspective.

On the other hand, while the theater audience of the play may be locked into one viewing position, without the alignment of the camera their vision is free to roam over the playing area, indeed over the audience area, making the performance in this venue a highly communal experience and prompting the insight that Krapp's condition is a condition shared by all. And as Bennett points out, the communal "live presence" of audience and actor found only in the theater introduces the possibility of altering the performance, even simply by coughing or rustling. In this situation, the actor's vulnerability helps generate the impression of Krapp's vulnerability. Because such effects are based on the premise of a shared "live" experience in a public space without the intervention of a mediator like a camera, the television version of *KLT* cannot come close to replicating them.

Despite the way theater places the audience and the play in the same physical space, the audience and Krapp do not, however, share a parallel space: Krapp is in his room (a private setting); we are in ours (a public building). On the other hand, in the television version, the viewer and the play are not located in the same physical space or shared "live presence," but the viewer and Krapp do occupy a parallel space: both are in their room (a private setting). If one wanted to focus on the play's atmosphere of aloneness, the televisual space offers a better venue than the theatrical, simply because it not only eliminates coughing and rustling, creating a completely dead quiet space, but also because it does place Krapp and the viewer (usually) alone in this parallel setting.

Indeed, because television does not offer the communal experience or space of theater, rather than generating the insight that *all* experience Krapp's condition, the television version suggests that *one* experiences Krapp's condition, a less universalist and more postmodernist ethos. To really enhance this notion of being alone, ideally the television play should be run with no one watching, although of course this is impossible if we are to have a performance. Nevertheless, perhaps it is this impression of pure, unadulterated aloneness that so disturbed Cluchey in playing Krapp for television, expressed from the actor's viewpoint as a feeling of playing to no one. Ironically, the actor's solitude can also be understood as the perfect form of method acting for creating Krapp's character. Certainly, though, it is because of the ability to record the performance on videotape, and thus repeat it at will, and the lack of "shared presence" found in televisual discourse that allows one to watch this version of the play, alone, and in the private space of the home.

What the above discussion of the theater and television versions of *KLT* ultimately illustrates is a point made very early in the history of media studies by Stuart Hall, who was reporting on television to UNESCO in 1971: "even when television seems content simply to reproduce a theatre play in its original terms[,] the production has, in some way and to some degree, been rethought/reworked/realigned for television transmission" (4). This is true because the representational systems of theater and television are based on the broad, differing grounds discussed above, which means that a precise ontological "fit" cannot occur. One medium is not perfectly translatable to another. Hall's statement is also relevant to film and theater: when film and theater try to reproduce television or each other, they rethink, rework, and realign the other according to their own grounds. Thus the films *The Running Man* and *Interview with the Vampire,* for instance, contain a television show and a theater piece respectively, but always within the context of the signifiers of film footage. Nevertheless, without twisting Hall's words too much, the opposite notion can also be true: while the fundamental grounds of the media may remain particular to each, when one medium incorporates another, the narrative and structural principles of the latter may be used to affect the performance of the former. To return briefly to *KLT* as an example: watching the television version of the play is not the same as watching the theater version; but enough theater principles have been incorporated into the television production to make the experience of watching television *KLT* not the same as watching the usual TV broadcast style and format either.

In other words, one medium's narrative discourse and structural elements can also profoundly alter the narrative and structural principles of another. Theater and film can simulate the discourse of television with its characteristic segmentation and repetition, for instance, to a fascinating degree: *The Running Man* uses a game-show formula as well as segmentation and juxtaposition, while *Groundhog Day* is based not only on the ability to repeat perfectly, a feature of videotape fully realized by televisual signification, but also on the notion that certain lives—the characters in advertisements, in syndicated sitcoms, or in archival footage (Princess Diana, for instance)—are endlessly re-livable. Both of these films, though, still ground the televisual features within the context of a highly causative filmic narrative and single, coherent text.

Similarly, a number of plays and productions clearly attempt to simulate the properties of televisual discourse. *Lesbians Who Kill* by Split Britches indicates in its opening stage directions that the lighting effects should produce the impression of a television set (186), and certainly the fragmented nature of the play in performance appears to reproduce television's segmentation. Megan Terry's *Home: or, Future Soap* offers a perfect example of how a televisual principle like segmentation may be deliberately brought over to theater. Because the play was originally written and produced as a teleplay in 1967 for Channel 13 in New York (Jordan 5), it has certain characteristics in its form and content that are particular to television. For instance, on the formal level, the teleplay is divided into segments rather than scenes, which perfectly utilize and reflect televisual assemblage, including the way it was shot—in segments out of sequence (Jordan 10). The structural segmentation, in turn, reinforces a cultural commentary about the fragmented condition of postmodern life, of which television is at least a symptom. In addition, the teleplay uses television sets to comment on the surveillance and control of people even in their own *home*. When the play made its journey from the small screen to the stage, rather than rewriting its structure as long, interrelated dramatic scenes, Terry retained the segmented televisual structure as well as its correlation to the cultural commentary.

Even if a play does not deliberately indicate in its text that a televisual discourse is being invoked, certain productions may situate themselves within this context regardless. For example, of the two productions of Tony Kushner's *Angels in America* that I attended, one was clearly relying more systematically on a televisually savvy audience, and rendering a more postmodernist interpretation of the script than the other. The production by the Intiman Theater in Seattle, Washington, used a relatively bare stage, set each scene as an individual Ibsenian "window," and made complete and rapid changes between scenes. The student production at the McLeod Theater at Southern Illinois University Carbondale, on the other hand, visually presented all of the scenes at once, spreading them across the stage and up the sides of the theater, and then simply switched the lighting from scene to scene as they were being played. Designing the set in this way not only well represented the play's already fragmented, soap-operatic narrative, but also gave the impression that the panorama of scenes simulated multiple channels, something like a televisual "super-flow." In this way, the SIU production incorporated television's sense of simultaneity, or the availability of multiple channels existing in its background and always available for viewing. Watching this production of *Angels* was akin to cutting a "viewer-flow" by channel surfing through the "super-flow" with the director in charge of the remote. No doubt this type of set design was intended to render a "postmodern setting," as the director, David Krasner, wrote in the play's program.

In fact, more than the filmic uses of television and theater or the translation of plays for television broadcast, I'm interested in the sort of theatrical performance of television represented by plays like *Lesbians Who Kill* and *Home,* and Krasner's production of *Angels in America.* What happens when drama performs television, when it incorporates televisual discourse into its structure or narrative form, when it allows television to occupy the same physical, theater site? What sorts of collisions, adaptations, and adoptions occur under these circumstances? And what sorts of theoretical implications obtain in the semiotic, performative, and spectatorial "grounds"? Interestingly, theater is unique among the media in that it is the only one that can allow the actual embodiment of another medium to occur within its physical environs. When film or television incorporate other media, the other media have to be first translated into electronic beams of light before they can be visually represented. For this reason, film and television appear to absorb other media more completely into their performative grounds. On the other hand, a television set or film screen sitting on a stage still has its physical integrity even though it has also become a theatrical signifier—an icon—within the language of the play's set. This ability to embody physically another medium has two effects. First, it allows the theatrical signification to be highly transparent. While a television set on stage may be a representation of a television set, it is also likely to be seen as just a television set. Second, it allows the incorporated medium to retain a certain amount of performative integrity. This integrity makes possible the purest form of what Jensen calls *"structural* intertextuality," or the use of one medium within another (120).

But how is theater able to do this? How is it able to structurally integrate into its space another medium such as television? Structural intertextuality in theater is built on the notion of rupture, the ability to break apart the chains of signifiers. The trace between difference and deferral—the trace that Jacques Derrida terms *différance*—constitutes a weak link in signification. In theater, it is possible to break physically this weak link, and enfold into it some other signifier or even an entirely different semiotic system. The rupture of the trace makes theater a truly interruptible medium, even more so than television. I have argued elsewhere that the television "megatext" or flow is based on the notion of interruption, and indeed it is as a narrative impulse. But once television's programs have been inserted into the channel flow, there is no way to break apart physically the televisual signifiers. Although channel surfing or simply switching off the television set appear to be ways to interrupt television, they are really just ways to interrupt "reading" and do not actually affect the television broadcast.

Theater on the other hand, as Bennett has pointed out, can indeed be physically affected, even stopped in mid-performance. The traditional theater has always worked hard to minimize this vulnerability in signification, and everyone from the actors to the audience is trained to ignore anything that might interrupt the performance and to keep going no matter what. The avant-garde theater has at times exploited this vulnerability by inviting, even instigating, the audience to insert some signifiers of its own into the performance—Peter Handke's *Offending the Audience,* for instance. Indeed, the rupture of its signifiers gives theater its own form of open-endedness, if we think of the signifiers as being like the numbers of the number line. While the television series may be based on the notion of infinity at the end of the number line, theater is based on the notion of infinity between the numbers (what mathematicians term "virtual infinity"), the fact that one can always locate another number between any two.[1]

Pavis cites repetition, as I mentioned earlier, as well as improvisation as two ways the theatrical avant-garde "tries to free itself from the sign, but always succumbs to it in the end" (182). It is, of course, impossible for theater to free itself from signification or to defeat it, because theater is by definition a semiotic enterprise. However, plays that incorporate televisual discourse perhaps offer a third option in attempting to deal with the limitations of theatrical signification—and that is to manage the signifiers in new ways. In the process, they also generate certain theoretical implications about performance. And it is, of course, because of the rupture of theatrical semiosis that such a trial and its implications can take place.

The structural intertextuality that theater is thus able to allow to another medium like television means that all sorts of characteristics that typically belong to television can become part of, and indeed alter, the semiotic and structural functioning of theater. For example, there is the matter of speed. According to Bert O. States, "theater . . . must process time at the speed of the actor's body" (76), a statement that is intuitively correct. Because Hamlet, for instance, is embodied in the real person who plays him, he would seem to be limited to moving at the pace of the real person. But what happens when a television monitor with a videotape and fast forward, rewind and slow motion controls is placed on stage and makes up part of the performance? What happens when Hamlet or the play *Hamlet* is represented to some extent on a television monitor? In fact, *Hamletmachine* by Heiner Müller allows an examination of this sort of question.

Müller's play calls for three television monitors to be placed on the stage in part 4, but the stage directions do not specify what should be run on the monitors, if anything at all. In a classroom experiment, I asked the members of my graduate seminar to play director by bringing to a workshop production of the play videotapes to run on the monitors. They responded with a fascinating array of material, ranging from video noise to television cartoons to advertisements to filmic performances of *Hamlet.* Indeed, at one point we had different versions of *Hamlet* running at different speeds on the monitors behind a student reading the corresponding live part in Müller's play. What this experiment demonstrated was that television is indeed capable of running at a different "RPM," of processing a different rate of time for the play than one finds in the live action. *Hamlet* on fast forward is physically impossible for live actors to simulate, and indeed *Hamlet* undergoes radical performative and interpretive change at this rate of speed.

At the same time, though, this experiment also showed that because the television monitors and thus the images on them are embodied in theater space, theater is not limited to processing time at the rate of live action either. The performative integrity that theater allows to television in its site makes it possible for theater to deliver portions of the performance at speeds available to the television medium. The character, Hamlet, for instance, may be processed at the rate of the actor's image, not just at the rate of his body. (And this means that some portion of the performance at least is now perfectly and endlessly repeatable, a feat that theater has never before been able to perform.) Similarly, Joyce Carol Oates's play *Tone Clusters,* which uses video rewind on its television monitors, demonstrates how postmodern drama can incorporate television to interrogate theatrical assumptions such as the forward progression of time in performance.

Certainly, the matters of speed or time are ways theater may be deeply affected by the structural intertextuality of television. And as the example of *Hamletmachine,* as well as *Tone Clusters,* demonstrates, it is actually at the semiotic level that these effects take place, because the televisual discourse is delivered within the context of the theatrical. It is only because the theatrical signifiers are so transparent in this sort of performance that we do not realize that what is being speeded up, or slowed down, or rewound are not just the televisual signifiers, but the theatrical signifiers themselves. But, one could argue, if the entire theatrical performance is still moving forward at a uniform rate of time, regardless of the speed or direction of action on the television monitors, are not the theatrical signifiers ineluctably tied to the rate and progress of "real" time?

To answer this question affirmatively would be to confuse the notion of time available to the theatrical signifiers with the audience's notion of time. Audience time or "real" time is, of course, always moving forward at the same biological pace. This is true whether the audience is watching television, a movie, or a play, and occurs regardless of what is being presented, or at what speed, or in what direction on the stage or on the screen. But the fictive world that is actually presented on the stage or on the screen is not limited to the laws of biology; because it has been constructed semiotically as representation, it is only tied to the laws of its structural elements, its internal logic and its methods of signification. In other words, because the theatrical signifiers are a means to representation, they merely *represent* time. They are not time itself. The theatrical signifiers are equivalent to clock time, and like clock time are able to run fast or slow, forward or backward.

Thus, the structural intertextuality of television in theater space exemplified by *Hamletmachine* also has some theoretical implications for understanding how theatrical signifiers work and the ways they may be differently manipulated, implications that are not obvious until television's properties are allowed to alter the theatrical performance. Although States's claim—that time in theater runs at the rate of the actor's body—is correct intuitively, it is wrong theoretically. Theater processes time at the speed of its signifiers, whether those signifiers are embodied by an actor or by some other imagistic form. Would it have been possible to recognize this semiotic principle without the performance of television in theater space? I suspect not. It is because the television monitor can actually show the theatrical signifiers moving at a pace different from the usual live action that makes principles like rate of time or progress as a function of semiotic manipulation so apparent.

Interestingly, the incorporation of television in a play like *Hamletmachine* also allows television to comment on another aspect of time in theater—anachronism—and again it does so through manipulating the "trace" of signification. Regardless of its "live presence" and use of the present tense, which give the illusion of present time, theater is always arriving performatively in the past. Each performance enacts a re-visitation of the past because the fictive world and the text of the play constitute the already said. The signifiers have always already been written, which demands a continual slippage along the trace from the present to the past, and which defers the play from being completely brought up-to-date. Performativity always implies this quality of being out-of-time, of being more contemporary than the dramatic text the performance is enacting, though it is most obvious in a play like *Hamletmachine* that is not only revisiting its own mise en scène, but is making a detour into Shakespeare's as well. While *Hamletmachine* makes the type of performance that is usually seen as updating a play, the word "updating" is something of a misnomer. "Downdating" would be a more accurate term, for everything about the performance— from the actors to the setting to the cultural context—is anachronistic with respect to Shakespeare's *Hamlet* and *Hamletmachine* itself. To recast a comment of Herbert Blau regarding Beckett's Hamm, this situation comprises "a signifying presence with no reality except as a *figure of speech*" (282). Certainly, the appearance of television in a play like *Hamletmachine* is a matter of bringing the anachronism of performativity, or the signifying presence of absence, directly into the foreground.

In fact, Lee Blessing's 1991 play *Fortinbras* is perhaps a better example of the way television may be used to foreground the anachronistic performativity of theater. Like *Hamletmachine, Fortinbras* offers a postmodernist allegorization of Shakespeare's play by speculating on Fortinbras's inability to meet Hamlet's dying injunction "To tell my story" and his epistemological turmoil over what constitutes truth. While the characters who died in *Hamlet* all return to haunt Fortinbras, the most interesting ghost is, not surprisingly, Hamlet, who first appears in Blessing's play as a huge eye and angry brow staring out at the living characters from a television set. *Fortinbras* has a great deal of fun with the notion of Hamlet's ghost being confined inside a television set, but offers one of the most ambivalent positions on television in drama to date. For instance, a remote-wielding Ophelia clearly enjoys being able to "mute" Hamlet while he is giving the "Get thee to a nunnery" speech. And yet this celebratory response to television goes hand-in-hand with a tropology that links television with the grave.[2]

Indeed, the characters are baffled by television. They do not understand its nature at all, referring to the television set as "a strange sort of . . . box" or "a box of light" (47, 38). All of the things we take for granted about television—its vastness and multiplicity, for instance—are completely foreign to them. Hamlet describes the world of television as being full of "countless ghosts. . . . Speaking innumerable languages. Dressed in fashions I'd never seen. Crowds of them. Multitudes" (56). The presence of television in *Fortinbras* is akin to plucking a being from the future and inserting it unexplained in post-*Hamlet* Elsinore, and without a doubt this anachronism is one of the most humorous and charming aspects of the play. But there is a more serious point being made: the televisual discourse and its relationship to the world of *Fortinbras* exactly and obviously reflects the relationship all theater performances have to the fictive world and dramatic text they are attempting to enact. In a sense, theater is bound to something like the compulsion to repeat, except with the impulse to go in the opposite direction. Whereas the compulsion to repeat brings the past into the action of the present, theater takes the action of the present back into the past.

Fortinbras is also a good example of the way television's properties may be used to manage theater's in new ways. The play does not simply utilize the television set literally to confine Hamlet, or even, as in the television version of *KLT,* to represent metaphorically the character's existential entrapment. Rather, until he is released into an actor's body later in the play, Hamlet is actually embodied on stage as the television set. He is granted some motility by being mounted on a TV stand with wheels, and unlike a "talking head" is able to engage in conversation with the humanly embodied characters.

Productions of *Fortinbras* usually use closed-circuit television to generate theatrical interaction between Hamlet and the other characters. This makes the scenography very similar to the uses of "virtual reality" in theater space, perhaps best exemplified by the University of Kansas 1996 production of Elmer Rice's *The Adding Machine*. Operating on the principle that both theater and virtual reality are "live," this production incorporated actors and television and computer technologies to immerse the audience in a "real-time," computer-simulated environment. As in *Fortinbras,* the production even experimented with creating an electronic "head," a "virtual agent" for Zero in the graveyard scene, but computer-generated rather than televisual in this case.

Interestingly, the notion of embodying a human being in this type of electronic form is something television itself has been experimenting with. The program *Burden of Proof* on Cable News Network (CNN) often includes a guest who is electronically "present," virtually "live," on a television monitor by satellite hook-up. Of course, the use of satellite hook-up has become common on news programs. But *Burden of Proof* is unusual in that the electronic guest is shown not only as the image of a close-up shot (head and shoulders) but whose body is also "filled in" at the studio by the television monitor being mounted on a pedestal. This "cyborg" is then more or less "seated" with the studio panel. The program is clearly attempting to re-create the electronic image in some sort of humanized form. Blessing is basically drawing on the same idea in *Fortinbras.* Television's electronic beams of light as well as its physical characteristics are being used to generate an "actor" on stage, who then simulates theatrical "liveness." In fact, bringing television's electronic beams of light into theater space allows the play to produce a different and highly effective ghost for Hamlet. He is truly like the ghostly figures on television who exist in a shadowy underworld only by the arrangement of their electrons.

The camera shots used for Hamlet on the television monitor are the most prominent way that Blessing uses television to alter the properties of theatrical signification. The shot list is written into the stage directions, and provides notation of when the camera should be in a tight close-up of Hamlet's eye or pulled back to reveal his face (30). Of course, one way to understand why such extreme close-ups are necessary is to realize that the image must be visible to the theater audience. Because the audience is not in a home setting and therefore not particularly close to the television set, Hamlet's eye must be enormous in order for the audience to be able to see it watching the live actors.

But more importantly, *Fortinbras* is attempting to use the camera in the same way the television version of *KLT* does, by taking apart the body (another form of segmentation), closing in on certain parts, and then manipulating their size. In fact, the size of the body's features are not only being manipulated, but they are being switched back and forth between sizes, from the eye to the face and back again. These effects are, of course, impossible to achieve with live actors. Without the televisual discourse in place, or some other form of camera work, the closest theater would be able to come to producing this style would be a use of masks; but masks cannot generate the same type of realistic representation of the human body, the simulated "liveness" available through television, or the rapid manipulation of images.

What *Fortinbras* demonstrates so well is that, even though television and theater "do" different things, because theater allows television performative integrity in its space, theater can "do" at least some of the things that television does. By embodying Hamlet in the televisual image and then employing a number of structural principles available to television, theater can make its signifiers perform like television's. Indeed, the incorporation of televisual discourse into the theater space of *Fortinbras* and *Hamletmachine* not only enables the theatrical signifiers to be manipulated in these unusual ways, but also implies that, because performativity is governed only by semiosis and not by the flesh, it has always been theoretically, if not practically, possible to do so. Recognizing that it always does "succumb" to semiosis allows theater to have a few new ways to do it.

Curiously, once it becomes clear that theater is a world of semiosis, a world based on signs, plots, texts, and the manipulation of signifiers, the commentary television makes of theater begins to run in the direction of spectatorial paranoia. According to Paul Smith in *Discerning the Subject,* paranoia may be understood as a structural feature of narrative, as well as its more common manifestation as a literary theme of delusions. Smith writes, "Paranoiac delusions . . . are delusions of interpretation

and fictionalization, formed to protect the ego from any alteration which might make it unwholesome, unlovable" (96-97).
Drawing on Lacan's theory of subjectivity, Smith claims that the
subject tries to expel anything, including its own divisions, that
threatens the illusion of wholeness and coherence, projecting
what is unacceptable onto the external world. Ironically, this
projection then creates a fictional universe that is menacing to
the subject, precisely because it contains all those "bad things"
that had to be expelled in the first place (see 94-97). Thomas
Pynchon's *The Crying of Lot 49* is perhaps the most celebrated
example of a paranoiac structure, for one explanation of the
novel's plot is that Oedipa Maas is projecting the plot(s) herself.
(Interestingly, an internal play, "The Revengers' Tragedy," is one
of the "plots.") Oedipa is not only caught in a semiotic web that
is threatening to her, but she may even be weaving the semiotic
web herself.

Television may be understood in a similar fashion. If its
multiplicity, vastness, and constant restlessness are equivalent to
the divisions, the "bad things" felt by the subject, then the
appearance of these elements in the narrative, what Ellis recognizes as the distinctive aesthetic of television, may be understood
as equivalent to projection by the subject onto the external
world. In other words, the fragmentation and lack of coherence
within the super-flow of television are projected onto a world
that has been created as a narrative structure and fictionalized
universe. And then, of course, this fictionalized universe is projected, or broadcast, right into our living rooms.

The act of watching television thus becomes an act of entering into a fictive projection. As in *The Crying of Lot 49,* where
Oedipa's fictive projection becomes the reader's, television's
paranoiac structures now belong to, and indeed vicariously
threaten, the viewer. However, because television is often
watched with casual attention and very likely is seen as part of
the background to home life, entering into the fictive projection
is a much less conscious act on the part of the television viewer
than it is on the part of a reader. This has the effect of opening
the viewer into something that seems *vaguely* threatening, a
faint, but constant, menacing presence that is difficult to pin
down. In fact, this act of projection by television with its uncon-

scious adoption by the viewer may be translating into the fear promoted by technological determinists like Jean Baudrillard that television is "overwriting" the world.

However, there is another variable in this equation of paranoia that can make the threat, certainly to many viewers, seem more overt: that is, the projection by the viewer of his or her own viewing subject position onto television. Television does not offer the possibility of direct communication, as the theater does. Because of the hard reflective surface—the mirror—of the television screen, only images seem to reflect back. But what if the mirror were imagined as two-way? Indeed, a two-way mirror stage is a common paranoiac fantasy of television viewers, a fantasy suggesting that somehow, in watching television, television is watching back. The recent film *The Truman Show* is an allegorization of this possibility, a paranoia exacerbated by the real possibility in our postmodern world of ordinary people being placed under surveillance in shopping malls, in banks, even "bugged" in their own homes. It also stems from the illusion of eye contact practiced by some television programs, in which the host appears to look straight into the viewer's eyes. The host becomes the other, the Sartrian "being-as-subject" who positions the viewer as "being-as-object." But on a more psychoanalytic level, it stems from the function of looking itself.

Looking is one of the primary ways divisions in subjectivity are formed and recognized. For instance, by looking into the mirror during the mirror stage, the subject gains a false sense of whole or coherent selfhood. Looking, therefore, has something to do with what is false, the "bad things" of the subject that must be expelled by projecting them onto the external world, in this case onto what is being watched. But once there, the "bad things" always return to discomfit the subject, here in the form of the watcher feeling as if he or she were being watched. In television viewing, the fact that what is functioning as an external world is itself already a projected, fictionalized universe only makes matters more intense, and heightens the viewer's paranoia of being under surveillance. Indeed, this scenario is actually played upon by some television programs. The crime reenactment show *Unsolved Mysteries,* for instance, invites viewers to spy on each other in the service of catching fugitives. Amazingly, it creates a situation in which entire communities, at the request of television, put themselves under surveillance, and generates the sort of anxiety that emerges from a climate of suspicion.

Several of the plays discussed above also dramatize a paranoiac scenario about television. For instance, *Home* contains a commentary about surveillance and its connection to television. By literally enacting a two-way mirror stage, the play projects the fantasy of being watched. The characters are not simply subject to the impression of being watched by the officials on the television screen, they are actually being watched via a television camera in their room. Moreover, the segmented structure of the teleplay as well as the stage version may be understood as the projection onto a narrative form of the divisions running rampant in the very soul of television. Similarly, in *Fortinbras* the huge eye of Hamlet on the television screen deliberately comments on the viewer's fantasy of being watched by television. But, interestingly, it also becomes part of a commentary on the workings of paranoia in the theater as well.

In a number of ways, *Fortinbras* is about paranoid fantasies: rather than tell the story of what happened in *Hamlet,* Fortinbras wants to concoct a different story based on the paranoia a Polish spy was able to instigate in the royal family (15). According to his logic, a spy would give the public an image upon which to project their hatred (33); this spy story may be Fortinbras's way of projecting in a narrative form the fantasy of being watched by Hamlet, or at least by his huge televisual eye. Indeed, the play itself may be interpreted as the projection of a fear of being watched by *Hamlet,* even in a sense of being watched by the author of *Hamlet.* All of these paranoias in *Fortinbras* deliberately draw attention not only to the problematic nature of the act of looking in television, but also to the act of looking in theater.

Like all the visual media, theater is about paranoia on some fundamental levels, though perhaps not as obviously because of the possibility of direct communication between the viewer and the viewed. As Barbara Freedman writes, paranoia is an important condition for theatrical discourse, especially connected, as it is, to the act of voyeurism and the fear "of being the object of a regard" (67). As in film, voyeurism in theater is a much stronger force than it is in television, and the relationship of voyeurism to exhibitionism has to be carefully maintained. Theater has to be under a regard without appearing to watch back. If this condition is not met, the illusion, or what Smith would call the paranoiac projection, of a coherent, fictionalized universe—the play-world—may begin to break down, and the ambiguities in the subjectivity of theater as well as its semiotic rupture become all too apparent. Some plays, of course, deliberately attempt to make this scenario happen.

But voyeurism, while a necessary element in the mainte-nance of a play's illusion, is also associated with the "bad things" of subjectivity on the part of the audience. Not only does it partake of the sense of falsity generated at the mirror stage, but it is also more directly connected with the emotion of shame. For instance, we have only to consider what happens when the voyeur is caught in the act of spying. In perhaps the most cele-brated section of his discussion on the phenomenology of vision, Sartre describes what it is like to be caught looking through a keyhole and the emotion brought on: "I shudder as a wave of shame sweeps over me" (369). In other words, the very act of looking practiced by the voyeur always carries the threat of shame. But because theater needs spectators, and therefore must sanction voyeurism—"it's okay to stare here"—something must be done with the shame. In fact, what theater ends up doing is offering to absorb the shame by allowing the "bad things" of the voyeur to be expelled onto its play-world.

However, the introduction of televisual discourse in a play takes away the ability of theater to absorb effectively the dis-turbing elements of functions like voyeurism. The televisual dis-course brings in the viewer's impression of being watched by television—the two-way mirror—so that the regard theater is under is turned back onto the audience. For instance, the look of the voyeur is circulated through the television screens and camera of *Home* and through the televisual eye of *Fortinbras* and returned to the audience. The voyeur gets caught, and the "bad things" that were once expelled return to haunt the audi-ence, just as Hamlet returns to haunt Fortinbras. But interest-ingly, the play-world is not as vulnerable to breakdown as it would be if the actors were to make eye contact with the audience. The presence of television enables the paranoiac impression of being watched to become part of the fictionalized universe of the play.

As one might expect, the televisual discourse engenders a vaguely menacing threat in this sort of performance, which is perfectly captured in Don DeLillo's play *The Day Room*. First presented in 1986 by the American Repertory Theater of Cambridge, Massachusetts, *The Day Room* is a play about paranoia and the paranoia that is theater. In the first act, a man named Wyatt is waiting in a hospital room for routine tests only to be repeatedly harassed by the inmates of the Arno Klein psychiatric wing who "dress up" and "act" as the hospital staff. The audience soon wonders if hospital life is being constructed solely around Wyatt's ego, and in fact the suspicion that he is concocting a paranoid fantasy is confirmed by his hospital roommate, Budge: "Children sometimes develop a particular delusion. They imagine that everything that happens around them is taking place by prearrangement. Things exist only as they affect the child" (43).

Additional paranoiac structures are further introduced in the second act. Here, the actor playing Wyatt is not only wearing a straightjacket, but also is embodied as a television set, which operates as a clever, and literal, manifestation of the viewer's projecting his/her own "bad things" onto the fictionalized universe of television. Interestingly, the barrage of disconnected images and plots that television is "broadcasting" throughout the second act can also be recognized as a projection of television's own divisions onto a highly fragmented, but aesthetically typical, televisual narrative form. The two paranoid fantasies involved in television viewing are here neatly combined.

But the entire situation is vastly complicated by an audience who shows up to watch the elusive Arno Klein Theater group, a troupe who seems to take as its performance philosophy the fact that it is never seen. The audience, both on stage and off, is posed with a dilemma: the Arno Klein Theater group really exists, but no one seems able to attend, *and* it is a paranoid delusion. Interestingly, it is possible to resolve this dilemma by first considering that the Arno Klein Theater exists as *The Day Room*

itself. And, indeed, there is some evidence to support this interpretation.

The Arno Klein Theater does one play over and over, and
that night's performance is supposed to take place in the day
room of the psychiatric wing in a local hospital (88, 90). The
day room of the Arno Klein wing is the setting for act 2 (59),
and Wyatt as the television set represents the patients' "lonely
monologues bouncing off the walls" of the day room or, indeed,
the monologues of the actors who are confined to the day room
(25). Despite the fact that an audience, in attempting to attend a
performance of the group, always finds instead "No sign of Arno
Klein" (83), in this interpretation they find, ironically, plenty of
"signs" of Arno Klein in the form of *The Day Room* itself. And
finally, at the end of the play after the onstage audience has left,
Arno Klein does arrive only to turn into Budge and begin the
opening movements of act 1. This repetition is, of course, the
open-ended dilemma associated with both the television series
and the theatrical avant-garde.

The play has returned to its beginning to remind the audience of the paranoid fantasy of act 1, expressed more than once
in theatrical terms. For instance, Budge compares the paranoid's
delusion that the world is created just for him to a stage set:
"The set goes up, the set comes down" (44). In other words, now
it is possible to understand that the fictionalized universe of the
paranoiac is equivalent to the signs of the Arno Klein Theater
group, which are the signs of *The Day Room* and, ultimately, the
semiosis of theater itself. The Arno Klein Theater group does
indeed exist as the paranoid delusion that is theater.

Now it is only a short step for the audience to grasp the self-
scrutiny operating in the play, and to understand that the vague
threat exuding from the paranoia(s) of *The Day Room* is resulting
from the impression they are under of being watched. The act of
projecting the bad things involved in looking onto a world of
signs, texts, and plots is now turning back to remind the audience
that all along it has been watching itself perform the act of
watching. In fact, the play makes this point clear at the ending,
where, interestingly, television is allowed to have the last word.

The television describes how to make a "pinhole box
camera" for watching an eclipse of the sun (100). Because look-

ing directly at the sun can destroy the eyes, the pinhole box camera allows the viewer to look at an image instead, and thereby protects the function of looking. Looking, the television is saying, carries with it the seeds of its own destruction, and depends on some form of mediation to protect the viewer from destroying his or her ability to look. The televisual discourse is present to remind the audience that the fictionalized universe they have under their regard is absorbing the "bad things" of looking, the shame of voyeurism, and enabling the very function of spectatorship to proceed. But, ironically, the return of their regard by television works only because television is able to render the absorption by theater less effective. The televisual discourse in the play is warning the audience about the fragility of their own act of watching a performance, and allowing theatrical modification through a "pinhole box camera."

Plays about television are ultimately plays about drama, not only the functions of spectatorship and its necessary paranoia in theater but other aspects of dramatic discourse as well—semiosis and performativity. In fact, as the plays discussed in this chapter demonstrate, televisual discourse enables us to recognize how intertwined the three threads of semiosis, performativity, and spectatorship really are in theatrical discourse. Running counter to the dominant notion that television is simply a banal techno-product of Western culture (which nevertheless wants to take over the world), this chapter shows that television can generate for postmodern drama the opportunity to question and experiment with theatrical "grounds," to modify performative practice, to figure into the continuing project of rehearsing dramatic and theatrical subjectivity. Indeed, among drama identified as most avant-garde of the past twenty years are those plays that incorporate televisual discourse, plays by such radicals of performance as Split Britches and Megan Terry's Omaha Magic Theater.

Through the refractive lens of television, issues of generic identity in a postmodernizing world and culture, a world of signs, texts, and paranoia—what Blau in *Take Up the Bodies* calls "conspiracy theory"—may be examined, taken apart, and reprocessed. While the place of theater is able to create a transformational subject position for critique of the media culture, as shown in the previous chapter, television can create a transformational subject position for theoretical issues of performance as well. Perhaps this "cross-fertilization" produces a "break boundary," the term Marshall McLuhan borrows from Kenneth Boulding to describe the point when a system, because of contact with another, "'suddenly . . . passes some point of no return in its dynamic processes'" (qtd. in McLuhan 38-39). Certainly, as the next chapter will show, postmodern drama is very much a part of the world of television and the media culture and not just in terms of performance practice.

Notes

1. This is essentially Zeno's paradox: between 1 and 2 lies 1.5, between 1 and 1.5 lies 1.25, and so on. The paradox is that an infinite succession adds up to a finite measurement. Plays have this "virtual" possibility.

2. The television version of Beckett's last play, *What Where,* also links television with death. Here, the television screen forms the crypt-space for the corpse of Bam.

Works Cited

Bennett, Susan. *Theatre Audiences: A Theory of Production and Reception.* London: Routledge, 1990.

Blau, Herbert. "The Oversight of Ceaseless Eyes." *Around the Absurd: Essays on Modern and Postmodern Drama.* Ed. Enoch Brater and Ruby Cohn. Ann Arbor: U of Michigan P, 1990.

Blessing, Lee. *Fortinbras.* New York: Dramatists Play Service, 1992.

DeLillo, Don. *The Day Room.* New York: Penguin, 1989.

Ellis, John. *Visible Fictions: Cinema: Television: Video.* Rev. ed. London: Routledge, 1992.

Freedman, Barbara. *Staging the Gaze: Postmodernism, Psychoanalysis, and Shakespearean Comedy.* Ithaca: Cornell UP, 1991.

Gussow, Mel. *Conversations with (and about) Beckett.* London: Nick Hern, 1996.

Hall, Stuart. "Technics of the Medium." *Television Times: A Reader.* Ed. John Corner and Sylvia Harvey. London: Arnold, 1996. 3-10.

Jensen, Klaus Bruhn. *The Social Semiotics of Mass Communication*. London: Sage, 1995.

Jordan, Glenn. "Director's Preface to *Home*: Television Version." *Home: or, Future Soap*. By Megan Terry. New York: Samuel French, 1967.

McLuhan, Marshall. *Understanding Media: The Extensions of Man*. Cambridge: MIT P, 1994.

Pavis, Patrice. *Languages of the Stage: Essays in the Semiology of the Theatre*. New York: Performing Arts Journal Publications, 1982.

Sartre, Jean-Paul. *Being and Nothingness: A Phenomenological Essay on Ontology*. Trans. Hazel E. Barnes. New York: Washington Square, 1992.

Smith, Paul. *Discerning the Subject*. Minneapolis: U of Minnesota P, 1988.

Split Britches. *Lesbians Who Kill*. *Split Britches: Lesbian Practice/Feminist Performance*. Ed. Sue-Ellen Case. London: Routledge, 1996. 185-223.

States, Bert O. *The Pleasure of the Play*. Ithaca: Cornell UP, 1994.

Williams, Raymond. *Television: Technology and Cultural Form*. Hanover: UP of New England, 1992.

Worth, Katharine. "Past into Future: *Krapp's Last Tape* to *Breath*." *Beckett's Later Fiction and Drama: Texts for Company*. Ed. James Acheson and Kateryna Arthur. New York: St. Martin's, 1987.

4

TELEVISUAL SEX AND VIOLENCE

The topic of televisual sex and violence, surely one of the
hottest on the cultural and political scene, oddly enough is one of
the best ways to recognize the vibrancy of drama in a postmodern media culture. Plays that perform television, particularly
the most sexual and violent, demonstrate that drama and television co-exist in the territory of the media culture because they
share the position of being the objects of a "disciplinary gaze."
The long history of attempts to censor the performance arts,
which is focusing right now on television, suggests that as we
enter the twenty-first century drama and television are bearing a
similar subjectivity. Thinking of the problem of drama's identity
in this way opens the door to rethinking the relation of drama and
television as a negotiation of cultural positioning, which allows
issues like media sex and violence and the ideological codes that
support them to find a place for interrogation.

From the moment television entered the North American
household in the 1950s, it has been the subject of a vociferous
debate over its portrayals of sex and violence. This debate reached
such a boiling point in the early to mid-1990s that ratings for sex
and violence on most types of programming, news excluded, were
instituted. From a Foucauldian point of view, the television ratings system is the latest action in an ongoing effort to "discipline"
television in a manner similar to the way the human body underwent disciplining in the eighteenth century by "the meticulous
control of the operations of the body, which assured the constant
subjection of its forces" (Foucault, *Discipline* 137).

No one disputes the fact that television offers scenes of sex
and violence and, sometimes, even of violent sex. Unfortunately,
a prohibitive amount of time and money has been spent on
social science studies that are ultimately ill-equipped theoretically and methodologically in their charge to determine how

much sex and violence actually occur on television, and then to proceed to an evaluation of the extent of their effects, if any, on the behavior of viewers. And yet these studies, which fall into the trap Marshall McLuhan warned us of years ago of focusing exclusively on the content of the media, are having an enormous influence on the governance of a popular art form. I would agree with the direction Raymond Williams indicated early in the study of television, and that is to pay attention to television as a "particular cultural technology" (4). Televisual sex and violence rise out of issues of representation and mediation rather than content and ought to be taken as a given, not, however, for any essentialist notion of the inherent violence of human nature. Rather, just as paranoia is fundamental to spectatorship, as discussed in Chapter 3, sex and violence are fundamental to the modalities of representation and Western epistemology circulating in our ways of watching, especially the voyeurism and exhibitionism associated with the spectacle of the body.

The television ratings, as well as a number of internal systems of coding television, ought to be seen as prohibitions meant to control how and to what extent these functions of representation are graphically embodied in the televisual image. Certainly, they are meant to control the threat of anarchy rising out of television's particular structure and formal properties. This chapter, then, uncovers what actually constitutes televisual sex and violence. After a discussion of the disciplining of television, I offer a critique of the social science literature, focusing particularly on the sort of programming that has been most harshly criticized—situation comedies, reality shows, and dramatic series like CBS's *Walker, Texas Ranger* and Fox's *Millennium*. By reading them against a number of plays, I demonstrate that postmodern drama can position its subjectivity in ideologically subversive terms that problematize the issues of media sex and violence. Last, I discuss Jacques Lacan and Antonin Artaud, suggesting that what may ultimately be at stake is the viewer's desire for contact with "outbursts" of the Real.

As discussed in Chapter 3, any sort of activity of watching contains an element of surveillance, because as Barbara Freedman argues about the paranoiac in *Staging the Gaze*, whatever is being watched is necessarily "the object of a regard" (67). This makes cultural bodies with an audience or public sphere subject to a variety of censoring or disciplining positions. However, even though these positions tend to form the sort of ideological discourse John Fiske understands as supporting dominant social interests (*Media Matters* 5), the action of disciplining should not be attributed to any single cultural police force of ideological or political persuasion. The power that makes surveillance and discipline possible rather resides in what Michel Foucault describes in volume 1 of *The History of Sexuality* as "a complex strategical situation in a particular society" (93). Just as technologies themselves are developed within a complex of cultural forces— rules, institutions, public desires (Penley and Ross xiv)—so too discipline ordinarily departs from a complicated variety of sectors. This is very true of the societal and cultural powers that would censor drama, theater and performance art, and television and film, powers that operate from "innumerable points" on the political compass (Foucault, *Sexuality* 94).

Here are a few examples. In England as late as 1968 the government oversaw the censorship of plays through the offices of the Lord Chamberlain. Since the 1980s in the United States conservatives have been trying to ban the public school teaching of *The Crucible* by Arthur Miller, accusing it of a variety of sins from vulgar language to a promotion of witchcraft and Satanism (DelFattore 201). At the same time, the National Endowment for the Arts (NEA) refused to fund Holly Hughes, a lesbian playwright and performance artist known for her controversial sexual politics. And virtually every zone of the political spectrum has weighed in on the issue of sex and violence on television: Planned Parenthood, the Secretary of Health and Human Services, the conservative American Family Association and Christian Leaders for Responsible Television, corporate advertisers such as Chrysler, Coca-Cola and McDonald's, the U.S. Senate, the Attorney General, the Surgeon General, and a laundry list of governmental, health, and substance abuse organizations (Lowry and Schidler 628-29; Signorielli et al. 278-79).

Such attention to the regulating of drama and television clearly traverses the political landscape, and as Foucault points out regarding the sexuality of the individual human and social bodies, goes hand in hand with a flood of measurements, statistics, and interventions (*Sexuality* 146). This has certainly been the case with televisual sex and violence and the social sciences. Since the 1950s, innumerable social scientists have attempted to measure televisual sex and violence, and some early studies such as the Cultural Indicators Project are still going. The latest effort has been the vast undertaking by the Center for Communication Policy (CCP) at the University of California, Los Angeles, which released its report in January of 1998. This study was commissioned by Congress to assess the extent of violence on the four major networks—ABC, CBS, NBC, and Fox—over a three-year period from 1994 through 1997. The networks agreed to the study after Congress made threats to censor violence, impose a ratings system, and require V-chip capacity on new TV sets. Interestingly, the CCP found that depictions of violence on the four networks had declined over the three-year period, in 1997 singling out only the reality specials or "shock-umentaries" and two dramatic series, one of which has since been cancelled, as guilty of excessive violence.

However, a reading of the social science literature on televisual violence, including the CCP study, reveals a number of problems, which is especially troubling when those who would discipline a popular art form are using for evidence questionable research and analysis. Some of these studies contain an obvious political, ideological, or academic bias. Other studies demonstrate just how much controversy and sharp disagreement there is among social scientists, especially media effects researchers. Some believe that televisual violence affects real behavior, a claim based on cultivation, disinhibition, or arousal theories but no real substantive data, while others do not. Several studies use definitions that are absurdly broad, even counting verbal "put-downs" as violent. And many studies, especially the earlier ones, simply count instances of violence as if they were so many beans without regard to the immediate or overall context in which the violent scene occurred. But even those studies that do consider context raise concerns about how the context, and its effect on viewer behavior, if any, is being interpreted.

On the one hand, contextual studies often assume that television ought to reflect reality without regarding the problematical nature of realism and the fact that all television programs, especially the dramatic series, are closely following the illusory formulae of narrative and dramatic semiotics, form and genre. Of course, in real life no one can keep getting up after being repeatedly hit in the head, but in our mythic texts they can and do. Furthermore, insisting on this sort of contextual realism flies in the face of complicated attempts by the same social scientists, especially the disinhibition adherents, to distinguish "good" televisual violence from "bad" on the basis of program context: i.e., if the violent scene shows negative consequences such as the victim's pain and suffering or the perpetrator's punishment, it is considered "good" violence. In *reality,* though, a considerable number of perpetrators never receive the negative consequences of being caught or convicted. Moreover, these studies often judge the immediate context without considering that the negative consequences of a violent action may only be shown much later in the program as part of an overall theme or message.

To its credit, the CCP study has tried to correct this methodological fault by attempting to consider a program's overall context in its determination of the level of violence in individual scenes. Interestingly, though, the CCP study like many other contextual analyses is governed by an ideological subject position that not only assumes cultivation effects but is interested in applying the same, tired standard of middle-class morality that was used to repress or appropriate the "vulgar," lower-class blood sports (Fiske, *Understanding Popular Culture* 70). More specifically, violent scenes are judged, whether individually or in overall context, according to ideological codes that were initially developed to regulate the popular theater—the melodramatic rubric of the well-made play with its binary divisions of good guys and bad, good motives and bad, positive consequences and negative, and rewards and punishment (see for instance Potter, "Indexing Risk" 233-34 and CCP).[1] In a very real sense, this good/bad binary is a perfect correlation to the inside/outside binary, an ideological positioning that John Ellis sees confirmed in the televisual experience itself, where the comfort of the viewer inside the domestic setting contrasts starkly with the busy outside world depicted on the screen (166).

Imagine the pressure to conform that this sort of social science analysis together with corporate and political power must exert on television producers, especially when the ideological code is linked to the imposition of ratings and threats of censorship and boycott. Violent scenes end up being legitimated only if they are embraced by the binary formula dictated by unsubstantiated media effects research. Not surprisingly, this situation immediately limits any sort of overt opportunity for television to experiment with something like an aesthetic of violence, as Quentin Tarantino does in *Pulp Fiction* or as Artaud theorized. And indeed it is almost impossible to find a violent scene on television that has not been de-fanged by the appropriate dramatic form of the ideological codes. For instance, *America's Funniest Home Videos,* which is one of the most vicious programs on television, regulates its violent scenes—such as an obese woman falling off a horse or a man taking a baseball in the genitals—through the vaudevillian codes of slapstick.

However, what would be ironic if it were not so troubling about projects like the CCP study, and may account for the inability of the television networks to see eye-to-eye with social science research and other institutions over issues like media sex and violence, is their failure to apply coherently and systematically their own ideological code. This may result from the situation Raymond Williams recognizes of cultures that simultaneously applaud "authorized" violence but deplore "unauthorized" violence (116-17). For instance, the CCP study cites CBS's *Walker, Texas Ranger* as one of the most violent series on the four networks, in part because Walker and his surrogates do not receive negative consequences for their acts of violence. Yet the show is thoroughly melodramatic, almost cartoonish in its application of a binary formula, exuding middle-class politics to an astonishing degree of articulation. While it is true that numerous individual scenes in *Walker* are violent, mainly because the program showcases the star's martial arts skills, each scene is invariably contextualized within the ideological code of the good guys versus the bad, with the bad inevitably punished in the end.

In one recent episode, "Mr. Justice," a young prisoner is shot and killed while attempting to escape an army-style boot camp Walker has established as an alternative to sending young violent offenders to prison. According to the methodology of the

CCP and other studies, this scene would have to constitute "bad" violence, because it does not show the guard who did the shooting receiving any negative consequences or punishment. On the other hand, it does show immediately the negative consequences of shooting someone—the prisoner dies—which would be considered "good" violence. Within the immediate context, the scene also demonstrates the negative consequences—being shot—of refusing to trust authority figures and breaking the rules ("good" violence), while within the overall context, it fits into the general message that all actions have consequences: the death of the young prisoner is ultimately a result of his own previous violent acts (also "good" violence). Last, the scene is one of numerous examples in the episode that demonstrate in a very heavy-handed rhetoric to the other young men at the camp and the television audience what happens when we act irresponsibly (again, "good" violence). By my count, four "goods" to one "bad" ought to mean the "goods" have it. It is difficult to accept the CCP's charge against *Walker* when the program consistently legitimates violent scenes on the basis of the CCP's own ideological code and appropriate dramatic form. In *Walker,* violence is always "good" or "authorized" if it eventually works toward the general benefit of society, an ideology completely in accord with a culture that makes the same claim about the death penalty and war.

Similar observations may be made about the reality shows, the other area of television programming the CCP study highlights as excessively violent. These are television programs like Fox's *Cops* and *World's Wildest Police Videos* that rely on the videotape of real criminal acts. Interestingly, *Cops* is surprisingly nonviolent, being more about the day-to-day drudgery of busting petty criminals than any sort of glamorous shootouts. And the theme song to *Cops* should surely alert viewers to the ideological code the series works within: "Bad boys, bad boys/whatcha gonna do/whatcha gonna do/when they come for you." Similarly, while *World's Wildest Police Videos* does repeatedly show scenes of violence as the CCP study points out, the actions of both the police and the criminals are always embraced by the moral code of justifying the behavior of the good guys who are restoring law and order to a world on the brink of criminal chaos. In the discourse of the program, the bad guys are always "mad," "insane," or "berserk."

Moreover, the dramatic codes of these sorts of programs indicate that discipline flows out of self-discipline, internal televisual censorship as well as external cultural forces. Because the media are large market-driven businesses, television shows are subject to corporate practices that function as discipline even without the ratings threat, a situation hilariously allegorized in "Somehow, Satan Got Behind Me," a 1998 episode of *Millennium*. The Head of Broadcast Standards at a television network is eventually driven mad by his own efforts to regulate the violent and sexual content of television shows, and finally in a violent frenzy bursts into the filming of an alien autopsy scene and kills some of *The X-Files* cast before committing suicide. Because the camera has continued to tape during this event, the scene is circulated back into television programming as part of a reality show, *When Humans Attack*. This episode demonstrates that the act of disciplining television is actually more violent than any scene on television, a sort of blood sport in itself, because televisual violence will always be mediated by the disciplining codes of some ideological, corporate, or dramatic agency of broadcast standards.

The disciplining of television regarding sexual content is just as problematic. In this case, social scientists often differ in their interpretation of essentially the same data base. For instance, in comparing 1979 to 1989, Barry Sapolsky and Joseph Tabarlet conclude that sexual content on television did not diminish over the ten-year period, while in following the years 1987 to 1991, Dennis Lowry and Jon Schidler find a substantial decrease. As in the violence studies, cultivation theories have promoted the belief that sexual content on television does influence viewer behavior, an assumption that legitimates the FCC's regulation of television "broadcast indecency," even though as Edward Donnerstein et al. point out the evidence does not support this conclusion (115).

Actually, the censorship of sexual content by the FCC is just the most overt way televisual sex is regulated. Like televisual violence, sexual content is formally handled by the imposition of semiotic codes, mostly verbal rather than dramatic formulae in this case. In the Sapolsky and Tabarlet study, researchers discovered that most of the sexual content on television between the years of 1979 and 1989 was in the form of verbal innuendo in situation comedies and other humorous formats (511). Here, sex is constantly talked about but never "done." Far fewer instances of sexuality took place in serious programming like dramas, where presumably sexual activity would be simulated by the visual image and therefore recognized as much more dangerous than the suggestive remark. Because verbal language is a symbolic rather than an iconic semiotic system, it mediates and sanitizes sexuality much more thoroughly than does the visual image, and hence controls it to a greater degree. Indeed, if the sexual body is visually showcased on television at all, it tends to appear in arenas such as advertisements and sports, where it can be legitimated by an entire coding system of oblique reference. Such mediations as dance in advertisements and the accepted customs of athletic events (the stance of women gymnasts, the grappling of football, hockey, and boxing) enable the bodies to move, flirt, pose, or touch without appearing to engage sexuality. A great boon to corporate advertisers who want to sell products by selling TV images but without offending the prudes, the body becomes a pure fetishized object in its isolation, being displayed sexually but de-sexualized at the same time.

And last, a glaring problem of the social science literature on sex and violence is that only a few of the most recent studies admit any sort of viewer agency. For the most part, viewers are taken as completely passive blank slates upon which television writes its violent and sexual directives (or for television read theater and performance art). Media effects research is particularly guilty of seeing viewers as little more than robots primed to enact in real life what television shows them in fiction.[2] Viewer skepticism, intelligence, interpretative ability, or self-determination rarely enter the equation in any meaningful way at all. This is really quite an ironic oversight considering the active but strangely paradoxical role the public viewership plays in the disciplining of television. On the one hand, the public's anxiety over televisual sex and violence has been one of the agencies hardest at work in fueling the social science studies and in demanding a ratings system and V-chip legislation; but on the other hand, the public's demand for televisual violence has made the shock-umentaries among the most highly rated programs currently on network television (CCP). Whether pressuring Congress or wielding the remote, the viewer has tremendous power.

What the flawed nature of the social science literature ultimately demonstrates is the complexity of televisual discourse, a subversiveness within the medium itself, and the reductiveness of our understanding. As Constance Penley and Andrew Ross courageously admit, "we know very little about the uses and purposes that modern television serves in people's lives" (xiv). In fact, some of the contradictions and failures in the studies are not only a product of limited understanding, but occur simply because of ruptures in the act of disciplining, in applying regulations, and in the semiotic and dramatic codes. I would propose that televisual sex and violence occur because they inhere in the principles of representation of the visual arts, functioning in large part as the availability of the Real (which I discuss later in the context of Lacan and Artaud) and as graphic expressions of the viewer's voyeuristic gaze and the exhibitionism of the fetishized body, the latter two aspects much theorized and problematized by film and theater critics from Laura Mulvey to Judith Mayne and Barbara Freedman. In fact, sex and violence are connected indelibly just to the act of looking, and can even be found in common phrases such as the "piercing" or "penetrating gaze."

This sort of fetishizing gaze, moreover, has been built into the epistemology of Western culture at least since the Renaissance, which privileges vision as the primary rational field according to McLuhan (*Medium* 44-45) and as the primary will to knowledge according to Jacques Derrida (4). Visuality has been a Western passion since the discovery of perspective in art, the proscenium stage in theater, the telescope in science, and anatomical dissection in medicine. In this epistemological paradigm, objects are placed under a "penetrating gaze"—even cut open or mutilated to get a better look—for the purpose of gaining knowledge about them. The modern practice of *performing* an autopsy exemplifies perfectly how epistemology is connected to the act of looking, the word "autopsy" meaning "a seeing for oneself" [auto + *opsis*]. By opening the body—a violent act in itself—one can see and understand the cause of death.

Of course, televisual voyeurism is not as thorough or as spindling a gaze as, for instance, the act of watching a play or film. As John Ellis points out, because of the casual nature of television viewing, the "glance" rather than the sustained stare better describes the act of watching television (163). However, even the glance, which can itself be lengthy, maintains the fundamental subject/object positioning of viewer and viewed, the sexuality and violence inhering in the act of penetrating with the look, and the desire for knowing that goes along with it.

Indeed, the playwright Rosalyn Drexler was able to concretize the underlying functions of sexual content on television long before the widespread application of visual theories to the media and during a time of highly priggish management of televisual sex. Her 1966 play, *Softly, and Consider the Nearness,* allegorizes the erotic positioning of the television viewer by operating on the premise that the very act of watching television, regardless of the gender of viewer or viewed, involves a secret and private pleasure—a scopophilic gaze. The play depicts the love affair of a woman and her TV set, a relationship full of caresses, sexually symbolic behaviors, and lovers' discourse. In a way that interrogates the positioning of women in film understood by classic feminist film theorists, Drexler's placement of the woman character as voyeur makes the exhibitionistic body of television the literal "object of [her] desire" (Drexler 193), and this relationship between seer and seen plays on the epistemological pun of "sexual knowing."[3] Interestingly, violence also enters the picture at the play's ending, but in a way that subverts the claim that television breeds violence in the real world. When an armed burglar breaks into the woman's home, the TV set turns itself on just at the right moment to avert a catastrophe. The political point here is that violence in the real world can be undercut by television, a point that also politically positions the subjectivity of drama as an ally, rather than as a competitor, of television. Because the play also allegorizes the looking functions in theater between audience (seer) and play (seen), a subversion of the general ideological consensus about media sex and violence also takes place.

Furthermore, the nature of representation in the particular structure of television has also been identified, perhaps unconsciously, by numerous critics as fundamentally violent and sexual with its "Bombardment of Signs" (Collins 331) and "Z-axis," which Margaret Morse describes as acting "like a *skewer* or *pin*" (16; emphasis added).[4] Despite Raymond Williams's important notion of television flow, under TV's glittering surface lies a subtext of anarchy—Paul Smith's narrative paranoia (see Chapter 3)—the possible release of which was made explicit in the recent film *Stay Tuned*. Here, a "hellish" televisual discourse runs mad, insane, or berserk, threatening the smooth functioning of the mediating codes and the peaceful inside world of the television viewer. In fact, this threat punctures the surface whenever a program is interrupted for the commercial "break" or whenever the viewer channel-surfs, both of which demand constant accommodation by network programming.

Because sex and violence are already present in these characteristics of televisual representation, any codes that would scour television of sexual and violent images will always already be sabotaged, as illustrated in the Drexler play, whether they are instigated by studies like the CCP report or by the semiotic, dramatic, or mediating languages of television itself. In fact, the semiotic and dramatic codes are characterized by this internal contradiction, a state I will term "mis-regulation." Mis-regulation suggests that a collapsing binary has made the codes both agencies and saboteurs of discipline, simultaneously embodying regulating and disrupting forces.

The above-described episode of *Millennium* again serves as a good example of how mis-regulation can occur on television. *Millennium* is governed by the melodramatic code which positions Frank Black as the "good" and the serial killers as the "bad." In "Somehow, Satan," the "bad" is personified as four devils. However, this time the "bad" is not defeated at the end of the episode, because defeating the devil would put a permanent end to the notion of evil. Instead what it produces is an ambivalence, both a melodrama and an anti-melodrama, both the agency of ideological control and its subversion. Interestingly, "Somehow, Satan" not only comments on itself, but accurately depicts the general functioning of mis-regulation, for even melodramatic series that do manage to defeat the "bad" at an episode's ending have to re-produce the "bad" the following week. Engaging in this sort of "doing" and "looking" brings to mind what Timothy Murray terms the "theatricality of the van-guard, the performative watching over and judging of the fore and front part of the cultural thing" a characteristic "inherent in the televisual" (226), and in the case of "Somehow, Satan," specifically focused on the issue of discipline.

Certainly, I would argue that plays containing a commentary about television, especially if they make television the target of a censuring point, are necessarily involving the "theatricality of the van-guard," focusing on and playing out the ambivalence of mis-regulation. For instance, *Buck* (1983) by Ronald Ribman, a play about a TV crime simulation program, at first glance seems to draw a definite link between depictions of violence on television and violent behavior in the real world. However, by accusing television of collapsing the binary upon which distinctions of real and simulated violence are based, the play shows that the binary has collapsed for regulation as well, for the regulating effort is based on the ideology of binaries, in this case real/simulated rather than good/bad.

Similarly, in depicting a TV interview with the parents of a murderer, the play *Tone Clusters* (1991) by Joyce Carol Oates initially indicts the TV shock-umentary for its exploitative and voracious coverage of violence in the real world. But by the end of the play, a far less regulatory position has been worked out, one that acknowledges the contingency of human behavior. In *Motel* (1965) by Jean-Claude van Itallie, violent music on the TV set may be interpreted as the discursive background for violence in the motel room. However, any cause/effect binary that the play establishes is undercut when the TV set is smashed, itself becoming the object of violence in the play's depiction of "real" violence.

Coming Attractions (1980) by Ted Tally, which I discussed in the Introduction, criticizes the public's demand for the cult of the commodity serial killer and the media culture for meeting it. And yet the play, in its most disciplinary moment, "broadcasts" the execution of Lonnie on live coast-to-coast television. A similar mis-regulating project occurs in Tally's adapted screenplay of

The Silence of the Lambs, for which he won an Academy Award. Here, the viewer's fetishization of the cannibalistic Hannibal Lecter is engendered by the filmic process of creating fascinating visual images. Certainly, the Oliver Stone film *Natural Born Killers* (1994), which accuses television of glamorizing violence, does so through the delivery of its own glamorous, violent images. Of course, the deconstructive impulse in all of these examples brings to the foreground the realization that dramatic discourse itself is always undergoing the mis-regulation of discipline as the object of ideological control. In writing of performance art, Murray argues that the theatricality of the van-guard can indeed "challenge the broader cultural and political program of the regulation of performance as art" (230-31). Certainly, the effort by the above examples to negotiate televisual violence enables theater and film to perform depictions of violence.

The CCP's complaint of excessive violence in *Walker, Texas Ranger* is a perfect example of how mis-regulation occurs in the social science literature. The fact that the study fails to apply systematically its own moral code indicates that the moral code has already been sabotaged at the very moment of its disciplinary application. Ironically, it has undergone a subversion by the same violent scenes the CCP study dislikes most intensely and would most like to regulate—the showcasing of Walker's fighting skills. At the same time, the fact that the study lasers in on these particular scenes also indicates that a rupture is going on in the melodramatic code of *Walker* itself, most probably due to the excesses of the genre itself, "the visually articulated return of the ideologically repressed" (Feuer 115). Televisual violence produces a certain amount of leakage—a traumatic differend of the Real—which neither the moral code of the CCP study nor the dramatic code of *Walker* can contain.

In a similar way, the reality specials also undergo mis-regulation, most noticeably in their attempts to control the mad, insane, or berserk both in the form of the criminal violence and the threatening anarchy of televisual representation. But even while the binary codes are exerting discipline and mediating the violence, the visual image breaks through. As the networks know so well, it is not the act of disciplining that attracts an audience, but the explosion of violence in the semiotic code. This is certainly a point missed by the social scientists W. James Potter et al. in "Antisocial Acts in Reality Programming on Television."

Potter et al. wonder why the ideological codes are not leveraged even more extensively than they already are on television. Depicting higher rates of negative consequences, they argue, ought to make the viewing of televisual violence "a more pleasant experience" and attract more habitual viewers (87). First of all, viewing negative consequences is hardly a pleasant pastime, in part because they represent the "bad things" of paranoiac projection (see Chapter 3). It would have to be the rare viewer who could find pleasant the pain and suffering of a rape victim, for instance. Second, the act of disciplining, whether it be of television or human subjects, is also unpleasant to watch simply because it invokes the specter of punishment. In fact, the subversion of the disciplining act is precisely what makes the Drexler play so enjoyable, offering the sort of "pleasure" Fiske identifies as an escape for the body from the controls of culture (*Understanding Popular Culture* 94). Last, the violence and sexuality already inhering in the codes as well as their drive toward mis-regulation suggests that the attraction for the viewer must occur at some other, more urgent level. As Steven Shaviro claims in *The Cinematic Body* about the fascination of film (54-55), I would argue that images of sex and violence on television, rather than appealing to the more superficial level of behavior, strike at the level of the viewer's viscera, producing a "gut response."

Often identified as catharsis, this sort of response underpins the most popular—and long-standing—social science and literary defense of sexual and violent images in art and literature. In the case of television, sexual and violent content are seen as providing a social benefit by enabling the viewer a necessary opportunity to release pent-up emotion. But as Axel Honneth argues, following John Dewey's pragmatism, emotion is itself reliant on intersubjective recognition or mis-recognition, and is not simply expressive of some internal state (197). I would argue, further, that any cathartic outpouring is always preceded by something more basic and unsettling to all constructions of the social, whether they be human emotion, subjectivity, or ideology. Televisual sex and violence not only function as the graphic embodiment of visuality, but may offer in their most extreme expressions a sense of contact with the subjective and social breaching force of the Lacanian Real.

As Lacan theorizes, the Real is an order of disharmony and upheaval, a reservoir of traumatic differend that slides beneath the Symbolic and Imaginary registers, the sort of "hallucinatory icon" experienced by Bradley of *Yankee Dawg You Die* (see Chapter 2). Because it is beyond the construction of the subject, the construction of reality and the semiotic codes of representation, the Real is not accurately describable or directly accessible. Beckoning and eluding at the same time, the Real functions as part of the circulation of desire in semiosis, making it a necessary, if "lost," component of representation. It can erupt into the subject's world only *"as if by chance"* (Lacan 54), as the *tuché*: an encounter, accident, noise, outburst. Although little can be said about the Real, since it always engages the function of deferral in the Symbolic and the limits of human knowledge, one characteristic appears over and over in Lacan's discourse—a sense of the Real's violence.

This violence can clearly be recognized in the dream of the burning child, which Lacan takes from Freud's text in order to exemplify an encounter with the Real. The very words Lacan chooses to describe this dream are violent—"fatal," "terrible," "cruel," "firebrand," "fever," "burning," "death," "devoured"— and they are all directed at the body, whether the body is sleeping, awakening, burning, or dead.[5] However, the most violent moment in the dream is precisely the encounter with the Real, when the father is shocked out of his dream by the image of the burning body of his dead son, which calls to him, "Father, can't you see, *dass ich verbrenne,* that I am burning?" (58). In the violent image the subject encounters a traumatic leakage coming from a missed reality endlessly repeating, here represented by the father's terrifying return to a failure to watch over the son. Note also the emergence of the Real in the Lacanian field of visibility symbolized by "seeing" and "watching."

What sex and violence on television may offer is something akin to this image of the burning child, a violent, shocking encounter with the Real, a body-to-body rush that takes place deep in the ruptures of television and in the viewer's gut. Invoking some sort of return to what representation or the graphic expression is "hiding," the Real seems most available in scenes that are particularly explosive, like the horrific hallucinations Frank Black experiences in *Millennium,* the split-second visual and aural "screeches" that detonate in his mind and in the viewer's face. Moreover, because the Real belongs to the domain of the lack, each encounter brings with it the anxiety of incompleteness, the anxiety of paranoiac falsity installed at the mirror stage, and so the viewer enters the circulation of desire, which keeps him or her coming back for more and more glimpses of the Real. This desire, not the disciplining codes, is what produces the habitual viewer.

It is now possible to consider that the gaze of the television viewer which looks outward at the disturbing visual image, as the father gazes upon the image of his burning son, is also being turned inward by the visual image toward the viewer's own body, which becomes "awakened" by its own hormonal reactions (a function of the "two-way mirror" discussed in Chapter 3).[6] Given the title, this must be the intended effect of The Learning Channel's (TLC) prime-time reality show, *Adrenaline Rush Hour*, which features footage of horrible motorcycle crashes and severe weather. Surprisingly, such programming seems to have something in common with the sort of closed-circuit video art discussed by Margaret Morse in *Virtualities,* especially those projects that specifically invoke a body-to-body relation, a turn inward that involves and discomfits the viewer with his/her own video image. While Morse notes that this unsettling effect is hidden in the one-way mirror of television (171), I would suggest that sexual and especially violent content brings it precipitously close to the surface where the "subliminal energies" (Murray 235) released by the Real are realized in a physical rush along the edges of the viewer's body. In fact, such may be one of the most important effects of the televisual, which link it to the virtues of performance art: "to activate," as Timothy Murray writes, "the sights and scenes which performances always face, but never face, through psychic voyeurism" (235).

It is clear that, on the one hand, mis-regulation in the televisual codes attempts to control this turn inward, but on the other hand, it also swerves toward the sort of cruelty Antonin Artaud theorized for the "true theater," the highly sexualized and violent performance that shatters the social, that "disturbs the senses' repose" (28) and appeals directly to the body. Like Lacan, in *The Theater and Its Double* Artaud relies on a violent language to endow his discourse with a breaching force of its own, embodied in words such as "corpse," "shrieking," "delirious lunatics," "struggles," "cataclysms," "debacles," "battle," "melee."[7] In his tropology, the language and visual images of the "perverse" theater become acts of the body, "silent blows, rests, leaps of the heart, summons of the lymph" (27), which he compares to the plague. In a manner similar to the plague, the theater should push images to extreme limits in order to challenge the disciplining moral and formal codes that have taken the blood out of culture as well as performance. Here, I would argue, is the same connection Lacan makes of visuality to the Real in the "inflammatory images thrust into our abruptly wakened heads" (Artaud 27), just as it is in the image of the burning child brutally awakening the father. Interestingly, Artaud anticipated the criticism his theater of cruelty would spark—that violent images in the theater induce violent actions in the real world (82).

And, of course, for this very reason Artaudian cruelty would never be allowed to appear in its raw state on television and only emerges in the subversive functions of mis-regulation. Indeed, the cruel theater is barely allowable in theater, not however because the audience is tempted to behave imitatively, but rather because its violence and sexuality are so shocking. *AC/DC* by Heathcote Williams is just such a shocking play, a fascinating combination of the attempt to embody a violent Artaudian cruelty within the dramatic construct of a media culture, and get away with it on the stage. Set in the early 1970s, the play is a schizophrenic, hallucinatory storm of violent, sexual, and violently sexual images designed to disrupt the audience's complacency. But while it strikes at the audience with tremendous force, the play also savagely ruptures the disciplining codes of television and other media. *AC/DC* does not attempt to target television, even though reviewer Paula Kay Pierce read it as a technological deterministic criticism of the media. As Williams states in the introduction, "The play isn't against technology, but against its abuse by monopolies" (ix).

The play offers what Bert O. States describes as the pleasure of pain (see 200-213), or what Slavoj Žižek calls "horrifying *jouissance*" (180), a visceral experience in sex and violence that responds to a violent ideology observable in the media culture—and allegorized in *Millennium*'s "Somehow, Satan"—H. Williams's "abuse by monopolies." *AC/DC* suggests that this ideology not only controls television broadcasting but through it attempts to put viewers under surveillance and to discipline their bodies, the body being, as Klaus Bruhn Jensen claims in his discussion of television and the family, "the primary threat" (117). In the Artaudian economy of the play, the body responds in its most extreme, disruptive, contingent fashion—through its sexuality and violence. For instance, the character Sadie engages in violent masturbation in front of a bank of television monitors and glossy photos of media figures in an effort to rupture the ideological codes, literally invoking the limits of her body to demand, as H. Williams claims, "that the media be democratized" (viii). The play is terribly disturbing because it invokes unrelentingly the Real by throwing a barrage of "inflammatory images" at the audience right to the final scene when Perowne's head undergoes mutilation through the trepanning of his brain. In taking to a far greater degree the sort of hallucinatory outburst that occurs on *Millennium, AC/DC* makes it possible to recognize the power of theater to disrupt the ideological codes that would discipline the media.

Plays such as *AC/DC* show that television is very much undergoing the sort of disciplining action other media and other subjects have faced. But as I have argued in this chapter, the very act of disciplining is self-sabotaging, and is indeed another way the lens of scrutiny is turned inward to a self-scrutiny. In fact, plays that interrogate the disciplining of television are providing a way of looking again at theater. We are reminded that theater and theater audiences have also been subject to the same controls: the taboo against gay and lesbian drama in much of the earlier twentieth-century theater in America is just another obvious example of the ideological disciplining of theater. However, the history of theater as a highly censored medium reveals abilities to negotiate ideology that television is just now learning. In other words, theater has been mis-regulating for many, many years.

The fact that plays can now position themselves to make commentary about the functioning of ideological discipline comes in large part from the negotiation of subjectivity that has taken place between postmodern drama and television and the media culture in general. For the reason that it no longer occupies the place of primary mass communication art form, theater has negotiated a unique identity, gaining latitude for experimental and dangerous mis-regulations, even taking the swerve toward disruption to the extreme of de-regulating the ideological landscape. More than ever before, drama is in the position of "signaling," as Artaud would say, "through the flames" (13).

While drama and television share the place of the object of ideological discipline and surveillance, the characteristics of their identities as cultural institutions enable a vital conversation to go on about the media within the media culture itself. Looked at in this way, drama as a subject-in-progress is placed within a political alliance with other media. And as for sex and violence—they are enduring features of human and cultural subjectivity, visual representation, Western epistemology, the Real and the "bully blow" of new technology. But, as McLuhan reminds us, it is the place of the artist "to parry such violence" (*Understanding* 65).

Notes

1. I use a narrow definition of melodrama for the purposes of this chapter. For a broader definition that includes the televisual "operatic" style, thereby allowing all television to be classified as melodramatic, see Feuer 111-30.

2. An explanation for the tendency of media effects researchers to link closely real behavior and television may be found in Margaret Morse's comment: "Because 'live' media are temporally *engaged* or simultaneously transmitted and received, they seem, however speciously, to be more closely allied with everyday life and conversational flow than the authority of print or the detached realm of film fiction allows" (20). The same may be said of theater.

3. It is debatable to what extent film theory can be directly transferred to either television or theater. Certainly for those critics who

believe television markets to a female audience, classic feminist film theory does not readily cross over to television.

4. Morse describes the Z-axis as representing the depth of the televisual image. The X-axis equals width; the Y-axis equals height (16).

5. In the original text: "fatal," "atroce," "cruel," "brandon," "fièvre," "brûle," "mort," "dévoré."

6. Of course, this sort of bodily "awakening" is what the censors of sexual content want to discourage, in the belief that it leads to some form of sexual behavior.

7. In the original text: "cadavre," "en criant," "d'aliénés délirants," "luttes," "cataclysmes," "débâcles," "bataille," "piétinement."

Works Cited

Artaud, Antonin. *The Theater and Its Double*. Trans. Mary Caroline Richards. New York: Grove, 1958.

Center for Communication Policy (CCP). *Violence Reports*. Vol. 3. Jan. 1998. University of California, Los Angeles. 16 July 1999. <ccp.ucla. edu>.

Collins, Jim. "Postmodernism and Television." *Channels of Discourse, Reassembled: Television and Contemporary Criticism*. Ed. Robert C. Allen. Chapel Hill: U of North Carolina P, 1992. 327-53.

DelFattore, Joan. "Fueling the Fire of Hell: A Reply to Censors of *The Crucible*." *Censored Books: Critical Viewpoints*. Ed. Nicholas J. Karolides, Lee Burress, John M. Kean. Metuchen: Scarecrow, 1993. 201-8.

Derrida, Jacques. "The Principle of Reason: The University in the Eyes of Its Pupils." *Diacritics* 13.3 (1983): 3-20.

Donnerstein, Edward, et al. "On the Regulation of Broadcast Indecency to Protect Children." *Journal of Broadcasting & Electronic Media* 36 (1992): 111-17.

Drexler, Rosalyn. *Softly, and Consider the Nearness. The Line of Least Existence and Other Plays*. New York: Random House, 1967. 189-205.

Ellis, John. *Visible Fictions: Cinema: Television: Video*. London: Routledge, 1992.

Feuer, Jane. *Seeing through the Eighties: Television and Reaganism.* Durham: Duke UP, 1995.

Fiske, John. *Media Matters: Everyday Culture and Political Change.* Minneapolis: U of Minnesota P, 1994.

———. *Understanding Popular Culture.* Boston: Unwin Hyman, 1989.

Foucault, Michel. *Discipline and Punish: The Birth of the Prison.* Trans. Alan Sheridan. New York: Vintage, 1995.

———. *The History of Sexuality: Volume 1: An Introduction.* Trans. Robert Hurley. New York: Vintage, 1990.

Freedman, Barbara. *Staging the Gaze: Postmodernism, Psychoanalysis, and Shakespearean Comedy.* Ithaca: Cornell UP, 1991.

Honneth, Axel. "Integrity and Disrespect: Principles of a Conception of Morality Based on the Theory of Recognition." *Political Theory* 20.2 (1992): 187-201.

Jensen, Klaus Bruhn. *The Social Semiotics of Mass Communication.* London: SAGE, 1995.

Lacan, Jacques. *The Four Fundamental Concepts of Psychoanalysis.* Ed. Jacques-Alain Miller. Trans. Alan Sheridan. New York: Norton, 1998.

Lowry, Dennis T., and Jon A. Schidler. "Prime Time TV Portrayals of Sex, 'Safe Sex' and AIDS: A Longitudinal Analysis." *Journalism Quarterly* 70.3 (1993): 628-37.

McLuhan, Marshall. *Understanding Media: The Extensions of Man.* Cambridge: MIT P, 1994.

McLuhan, Marshall, and Quentin Fiore. *The Medium Is the Massage.* New York: Simon & Schuster, 1989.

Morse, Margaret. *Virtualities: Television, Media Art, and Cyberculture.* Bloomington: Indiana UP, 1998.

"Mr. Justice." *Walker, Texas Ranger.* CBS. 11 Apr. 1998.

Murray, Timothy. *Drama Trauma: Specters of Race and Sexuality in Performance, Video, and Art.* London: Routledge, 1997.

Penley, Constance, and Andrew Ross. Introduction. *Technoculture.* Ed. Constance Penley and Andrew Ross. Minneapolis: U of Minnesota P, 1991.

Pierce, Paula Kay. "Theatre in Review." *Educational Theatre Journal* 23.3 (1971): 343-44.

Potter, W. James. "The Problem of Indexing Risk of Viewing Television Aggression." *Critical Studies in Mass Communication* 14 (1997): 228-48.

Potter, W. James, et al. "Antisocial Acts in Reality Programming on Television." *Journal of Broadcasting & Electronic Media* 41 (1997): 69-89.

Sapolsky, Barry S., and Joseph O. Tabarlet. "Sex in Primetime Television: 1979 Versus 1989." *Journal of Broadcasting & Electronic Media* 35 (1991): 505-16.

Shaviro, Steven. *The Cinematic Body*. Minneapolis: U of Minnesota P, 1993.

Signorielli, Nancy, et al. "Violence on Television: The Cultural Indicators Project." *Journal of Broadcasting & Electronic Media* 39 (1995): 278-83.

"Somehow, Satan Got Behind Me." *Millennium*. Fox. 1 May 1998.

States, Bert O. *The Pleasure of the Play*. Ithaca: Cornell UP, 1994.

Williams, Heathcote. *AC/DC. AC/DC and The Local Stigmatic: Two Plays by Heathcote Williams*. New York: Viking, 1973.

Williams, Raymond. *Television: Technology and Cultural Form*. Hanover: Wesleyan UP, 1992.

Žižek, Slavoj. *The Sublime Object of Ideology*. London: Verso, 1989.

CONCLUSION

"But the true theater, because it moves and makes use of living instruments, continues to stir up shadows where life has never ceased to grope its way" (12). I would like to argue that Artaud's description has never been more accurate than when applied to the effort postmodern drama is making to grapple with television and the media culture. Such plays not only acknowledge the contemporary world and its "living instruments," but strive to respond, to critique, to contest, to celebrate, to exist in it. Like *Fortinbras,* they bring forth the shadowy ghosts of postmodern culture, its images and technologies. And like Artaud's theater, such plays are always groping for re-formulations of subject position, identity, and place in the media culture.

At the beginning of this book, I posed a series of what I consider crucial questions about the current viability of drama and its performance in theater, questions that pertain in particular to how drama meets the issue of its identity, its subjectivity, in a postmodern media culture. Certainly, the mesmerizing effect and overpowering presence of television has made our youngest medium still the most popular form of entertainment and the greatest purveyor of culture among the visual media today. And yet, like all the media arts (including drama), television exists in a complex of forces—cultural, political, technological, theoretical—that require constant attention and negotiation. Television, itself, cannot "perform" without its others.

Performing Television has shown that there is most certainly a viable place for drama and theatrical performance in the media culture. Apart from the theoretical necessity of "otherness," plays that incorporate televisual discourse generate an enormous number and variety of subject positions from which contemporary culture, including television, may be looked at, taken apart, critiqued, and celebrated. Drama forms a transformational site where issues of the media culture such as the

135

mediatized Imaginary may be interrogated. It forms a theoretical site where the "grounds" of semiotic, performative, and spectatorial theories may be challenged and developed. And it forms an intensely political arena for discussion of discipline and desire.

Moreover, as critics, scholars, and reviewers, we understand that the use of televisual discourse in the dramatic arts signals not an end to theater, but a means of looking again at theater and recognizing a vibrant negotiation with an other that enables subjectivity, in all its necessary incompleteness, to proceed. And there are certainly many more ways of investigating, analyzing, and appreciating this project than *Performing Television* has been able to incorporate. For instance: How is performance globalized in a televisual world? How does the media culture transform the ideology of a national theater? And how is televisual discourse interrogated in film and fiction, for instance in the movie *Pleasantville,* or Don DeLillo's novel *Americana*?

As play-goers and television viewers we need to keep in mind our political alliances. Because the underlying attitude in our culture still tends toward a puritanical distrust of performance, television has easily become the whipping boy of society (the scapegoat of teen pregnancy and school shootings) just as theater has for centuries. But if television is to reach the point of experimenting with and interrogating other media in the way drama has done, of stirring up shadows of its own, then a space of transformation for the (popular) artist has to be defended. Theater is not in competition with television, and can only benefit from recognizing shared interests and a shared place.

Recently, I heard someone on television ask the question, "what will replace television?" Because I was "glancing" at the time, I can only guess at the answer: "I believe in the future of computers? the Internet? virtual reality?" I suspect that the future of television, like drama and theater, has become less clear than it was in 1944, when *The Glass Menagerie* remarked on the future of television, as I noted in opening this book, and that we are already experiencing the beginnings of televisual negotiation with an ever-widening technological landscape. And as for postmodern drama and performance? We have only to look at the "virtual reality" production of Elmer Rice's *The*

Adding Machine at the University of Kansas or plays such as Gary Hill's *Soundbite* and Carol Mack's *Unprogrammed* to see that computer as well as televisual discourse is already finding a place in theater.

Works Cited

Artaud, Antonin. *The Theater and Its Double*. Trans. Mary Caroline Richards. New York: Grove, 1958.

INDEX

ABC 34, 114
absurdism 75, 86, 87
AC/DC 6, 128-29
Adding Machine, The 100, 136-37
agency 17, 20, 31, 53, 68, 73, 74,
  75, 80, 119, 122
alienation effect 59
Allen, Andrea 76
Allen, Woody 72
Althusser, Louis 58, 80n
America Hurrah 21n
American Daughter, An 53
American Place Theatre 61
American Repertory Theater 106
Angels in America 93
Annex Theatre 76
Arnold, Christine 69
Artaud, Antonin 112, 116, 120,
  127-30, 131n, 135
Astaire, Fred 65
As You Like It 32
Auslander, Philip 19, 47-48, 84
avant-garde 7, 94, 95, 107, 108

Bakhtin, M. M. 4, 27, 28, 49
Barbie 77, 79
Barnes, Hazel E. 30
Barr, Roseanne 66, 77
Battaglia, Debbora 56, 57
Baudrillard, Jean 21, 22, 103
Beckett, Samuel 7, 75, 87-89, 98,
  109n
Beckett Directs Beckett (PBS)
  88

Being-as-object 28, 29, 30, 36,
  38, 39, 45, 47, 103
Being-as-subject 28, 30, 31, 34,
  36, 38, 39, 40, 45, 47, 103
Belasco, David 54
Bennett, Susan 84, 85, 90, 94
Bergen, Candice 12
Berkeley Repertory Theater 63
Berkowitz, David 16
Birringer, Johannes 7, 8, 13
Blake, Warner 39, 46
Blau, Herbert 8, 14, 16, 98, 108
Blessing, Lee 7, 83, 98, 100
Boulding, Kenneth 109
Brazil Fado 21n
Brecht, Bertolt 21, 59
Breuer, Lee 21n
Brown, Murphy 12
Buck 21n, 123
Burns, Ken 60, 61
Butler, Judith 30, 31, 35, 44

Caribbean Imaginary 57
Case, Sue-Ellen 43, 50n
Cat on a Hot Tin Roof 34-36, 39,
  50n
catharsis 125
Caughey, John L. 55, 56, 59, 65
Caughie, John 56, 57
CBS 34, 114
censorship 111, 113, 116, 118,
  129, 131n
Center for Communication Policy
  114-17, 120, 122, 124

139

Chambers, Jane 7, 39, 41, 68
Chicago 21
Chickencoop Chinaman, The 61-
    63, 64, 66, 72, 75, 77
Chin, Frank 53, 61, 77
Chomsky, Noam 16
chronotope 4
closed-circuit television 3, 99,
    127
Cluchey, Rick 88-90
CNN 100
Collins, Jim 10, 121
Coming Attractions 3, 6, 7-20,
    21n, 123
computer 100, 137
Cops 117
*Corps of Discovery, The: The
    Lewis and Clark Expedition*
    60-61
cruelty, theater of 127, 128
Crying of Lot 49, The 102
cultural criticism 7
cultural Imaginary 56, 57
cultural studies 76
cyborg 100

Dahmer, Jeffrey 20
Davy, Kate 43, 50n
Day Room, The 83, 106-8
Dean, Nancy 41
DelFattore, Joan 113
DeLillo, Don 7, 83, 106, 136
Derrida, Jacques 94, 120
Dewey, John 125
Diana, Princess of Wales 56, 92
discipline 7, 16, 111-14, 118-20,
    122-25, 127-30, 136
Doll House, A 21
Donnerstein, Edward 118

Douglas, Mary 2
Drake, Sylvie 69
Drexler, Rosalyn 7, 121, 122, 125

Elam, Kier 84
Elliott, Anthony 31
Ellis, John 26, 85, 86, 102,
    115,121
El Teatro Campesino 68
epistemology 25, 29, 33, 36-37,
    39-40, 43-44, 45, 48-49, 71,
    98, 112, 120, 121, 130
essentialism 13-14, 18-19, 21, 25,
    30, 31, 43-44, 56-58, 62, 65,
    67, 72-73, 78, 80, 112
Esslin, Martin 7, 84
European Imaginary 57
exhibitionism 25, 105, 112, 120,
    121
expressionism 5, 69

facial reconstruction 65-67, 71,
    73
Federal Communications Com-
    mission (FCC) 118
Feldman, Jack 8
feminism 84
feminist film theory 121, 130n
Feuer, Jane 124, 130n
Fiske, John 113, 115, 125
Flitterman-Lewis, Sandy 59
flow, concept of 84, 85, 93, 94,
    102, 122
Forever Plaid 21n
For-itself 27, 28
For-others 27, 28
Fortinbras 83, 98-101, 104, 105,
    135
Foucault, Michel 111-14

Fox Network 114
Frayn, Michael 7, 32, 40, 55
Freedman, Barbara 26, 29, 84,
    104, 112, 120
Freud, Sigmund 43, 45, 126

gay drama 35, 129
gaze 18, 25-29, 36, 38, 40, 42, 49,
    84, 120-21, 127
glance 25, 121
Glass Menagerie, The 1, 2, 136
Gleason, William 21n
Glengarry Glen Ross 74
Gotanda, Philip Kan 7, 53, 63, 77
Green, Judith 69
Grotowski, Jerzy 2
Gussow, Mel 88

Hadary, Jonathan 11
Hajj: The Performance 21n
Hall, Stuart 57, 91
Hallin, Daniel C. 15
Hamlet 95, 96, 98, 104
Hamletmachine 4, 95-98, 101
Handke, Peter 95
*Handwriting, the Soup and the
    Hats, The* 55, 76-80
Happy Daze 21n
Herman, Edward S. 16
heterosexuality 35
high culture 8, 9, 14, 17, 31, 33,
    38
Hill, Gary 137
Holbein, Hans 34
Holquist, Michael 27
Home: or, Future Soap 83, 92-93,
    104, 105
homosexuality 35, 43
Honneth, Axel 49, 125

Hughes, Holly 113
humanism 19, 84
Hutcheon, Linda 15
Huyssen, Andreas 2, 20, 25
hyperconsciousness 29, 31, 32, 83

identity 1-2, 6, 18-19, 21, 25, 31,
    35, 39, 42, 44, 45, 48-49, 50,
    53, 54-55, 56-58, 59-60, 62-63,
    65-68, 70-73, 75, 76, 78-79,
    80, 83, 84, 108, 111, 130, 135
identity politics 54, 79
ideology 7, 16, 21n, 25, 30-31,
    34-35, 42, 43, 53, 55, 58, 60,
    63, 67, 68, 78, 111-18, 121-25,
    128-29, 130, 136
*I Don't Have to Show You No
    Stinking Badges!* 68-75, 76
I Hate Hamlet 21n
I Led Three Lives 47
Imaginary, the 26, 31, 42, 45, 47,
    54, 57-59, 60, 68, 72, 77, 80,
    84, 126
imperial Imaginary 56
information 8
international Imaginary 56
interpellation 67
Intiman Theater 93

Jackson, Michael 65, 66
Jameson, Fredric 1, 11
Jay, Martin 26, 27
Jensen, Klaus Bruhn 84, 94, 129
Jordan, Glenn 92

Kalem, T. E. 9
King, Martin Luther, Jr. 68
Krapp's Last Tape 88-91, 99, 101
Krasner, David 93

142   ·   *Index*

Kristeva, Julia 20, 26, 54, 66-67
Kushner, Tony 93

Lacan, Jacques 25-27, 28, 29, 31, 34, 36, 40, 44, 48-49, 57-58, 66-67, 102, 112, 120, 125-26, 127, 128, 131n
Laclau, Ernesto 25, 30-31, 49, 58, 80n
Last Summer at Bluefish Cove 41
Laughter on the 23rd Floor 21n
Laughton, Charles 71, 72, 73
LeCompte, Elizabeth 45
lesbian drama 40-44, 129
lesbianism 41, 43
Lesbians Who Kill 92, 93
Levinas, Emmanuel 50
Lewis and Clark 60
look, the 25, 28, 29, 38, 40, 42, 48-49, 58-59, 103-5, 107-8, 120-21
Lone Ranger, the 53, 61, 62, 64, 77, 78
Lowry, Dennis T. 118
Lynch, David 87

Mack, Carol 137
Madam Butterfly 54
Mamet, David 74
Marxism 31, 84
Mary Tyler Moore Show, The 76, 79
mass culture 2, 25, 33, 130
Maynard, Suzanne 7, 53, 77, 78
Mayne, Judith 120
M. Butterfly 54
McLeod Theater, Southern Illinois University Carbondale 34, 36, 93

McLuhan, Marshall 5, 7, 45-46, 109, 112, 120, 130
media culture 8, 14-15, 17-20, 21, 25, 37, 47, 49, 53, 55, 58, 63, 67-69, 73-76, 80, 83, 108-9, 111, 123, 128, 130, 135-36
media effects 114, 116, 119, 130n
media studies 8, 76, 91
mediatized Imaginary 7, 19, 53, 55-56, 58-59, 60-67, 69-73, 75, 77-79, 83, 136
megatext 3, 10, 12, 16, 94
melodrama 115, 116, 122, 124, 130n
Merleau-Ponty, Maurice 27
metadrama 55, 68
Metz, Christian 26, 47, 58
Millennium 112, 118, 122-23, 127, 129
Miller, Arthur 113
Minow, Newton 75
mirror stage 25-26, 37, 45, 47, 58, 59, 103-5, 127; two-way 103-5, 127
misrecognition (*méconnaisance*) 26-27, 30-32, 34, 36, 37, 39, 41, 44, 45-50, 58-60, 61, 64, 67, 77, 79, 125
mis-regulation 14, 122-25, 127-30
modernism 2, 11, 13, 14, 21, 25
Mohawk nation 57
Moore, Mary Tyler (Mary Richards) 53, 76-79
Morse, Margaret 7, 122, 127, 131n
Motel 123
Mouffe, Chantal 25, 30-31, 50, 58, 80n

Müller, Heiner 4, 7, 95-96
multi-media 7, 13
Mulvey, Laura 84, 120
Murray, Timothy 7, 8, 123, 124, 127

National Hockey League (NHL) 87
national Imaginary 56
Natural Born Killers 14, 18, 124
NBC 114
Nealon, Jeffrey 49, 80, 84
Newmark's Second Floor Gallery 46
Noises Off 32-33, 34, 37-39, 40, 46, 55

Oates, Joyce Carol 96, 123
objet a 26, 34, 36, 40, 41, 43, 44
Oedipal stage 26
Offending the Audience 95
Oliver, Edith 9
Our Town 3

paranoia 101-8, 112, 122, 125, 127
Pavis, Patrice 84, 87, 95
PBS 60, 88,
Penley, Constance 113, 120
performance art 7, 8, 13, 113, 124, 127
performative 7, 14, 25, 31, 44, 50, 63, 67, 73, 78, 80, 83-84, 93-94, 96, 98, 101, 108, 136
phenomenology 4, 12-13, 27-28, 38-40, 105
Pierce, Paula Kay 128
Playwrights Horizons 8
populism 15, 16, 18

post-feminism 77
post-Lacanian theory 25, 30-31, 36, 40, 58, 67
postmodernism 2, 8, 13-14, 15, 17-21, 21n, 25, 31, 34, 39, 46, 48-49, 53-54, 56, 74-75, 78, 80, 83, 90, 92-93, 96, 98, 103, 108-9, 111-12, 135-36
Potter, W. James 115, 125
Presley, Elvis 56
Puccini 54
Pynchon, Thomas 102

Quintessential Image, The 39, 40-44, 46, 68

Rabe, David 3
Rather, Dan 18
Real, the 31, 66-67, 112, 120, 126-29, 130
realism 5, 29, 115
reality shows 117, 118, 124, 127
Ribman, Ronald 21n, 123
Rice, Elmer 100, 136
Rivera, Geraldo 18
Roseanne 66, 77
Ross, Andrew 113, 120
Ross, Stuart 21n
Route 1 & 9 (The Last Act) 3, 45, 54
Rudnick, Paul 21n

Sapolsky, Barry S. 118
Sartre, Jean-Paul 25, 27-28, 30, 31, 36, 38, 40, 41, 44-46, 47, 103, 105
Savran, David 7, 35, 54
Schidler, Jon A. 118
segment 86, 87, 92, 101, 104

Seiter, Ellen 84
semiosis 7, 14, 17, 33, 34, 35, 43-45, 50, 55, 62, 83-84, 86, 93-97, 101, 102, 105, 107, 108, 115, 118-20, 122, 124, 126, 136
serial killer 8-20
sex 7, 111-14, 116, 118-19, 120-21, 122, 125-29, 130, 131n
Shakespeare 32
Shaviro, Steven 125
Shohat, Ella 56, 58, 67
Silence of the Lambs, The 20, 124
Simon, Neil 21n, 33
Simpson, O. J. 20
Simpsons, The 83
simulation 3, 21, 123
Sinatra, Frank 53, 65, 78
Smith, Paul 101-2, 105, 122
social Imaginary 56, 57
social science studies of TV violence 111-12, 114-16, 118-20, 124
Softly, and Consider the Nearness 121
Soundbite 137
Soup Talks Trilogy 46
spectatorship 7, 8, 18, 26, 58-59, 83, 84, 93, 101, 108, 112, 136
Split Britches 92, 108
Squat Theatre 13
Stam, Robert 56, 58, 67
States, Bert O. 4, 12, 39, 84, 85-87, 95, 97, 129
Sticks and Bones 3
Stone, Oliver 13-14, 18, 123
structural intertextuality 94-97
subjectivity: drama 6-7, 18, 25, 31-41, 44-49, 53, 80, 83, 105,

108, 111-12, 121, 129, 135-36; human 8, 18-20, 26-31, 34-36, 42-45, 48-49, 55-59, 61-79, 102-3, 105, 125, 130; television 111, 129
Sunshine Boys, The 33, 36-37
surveillance 92, 103-4, 112-13, 129, 130
Sussman, Bruce 8
Symbolic, the 26, 31, 42, 45, 72, 126

Tabarlet, Joseph O. 118
Tally, Ted 3, 123
Tarantino, Quentin 116
technological determinism 17, 21n, 73-74, 103, 128
Terry, Megan 5, 7, 21n, 83, 92, 108
That Girl 76, 78-79
Theater and Its Double, The 127-28
Thomas, Marlo (Ann Marie) 76-79
Tommy Allen Show, The 5
Tone Clusters 96, 123
Tonight Show, The 12, 29
True-real 66
TV 21n
Twin Peaks 87

University of Kansas 100, 137
Unprogrammed 137

Valaskakis, Gail 57
Valdez, Luis 7, 53, 68
van Itallie, Jean-Claude 21n, 123
video 7, 8, 127
violence 7, 18, 74, 78, 111-30